MOON

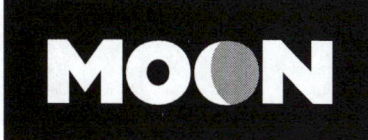

ZAGREB & LJUBLJANA

SHANN FOUNTAIN ČULO

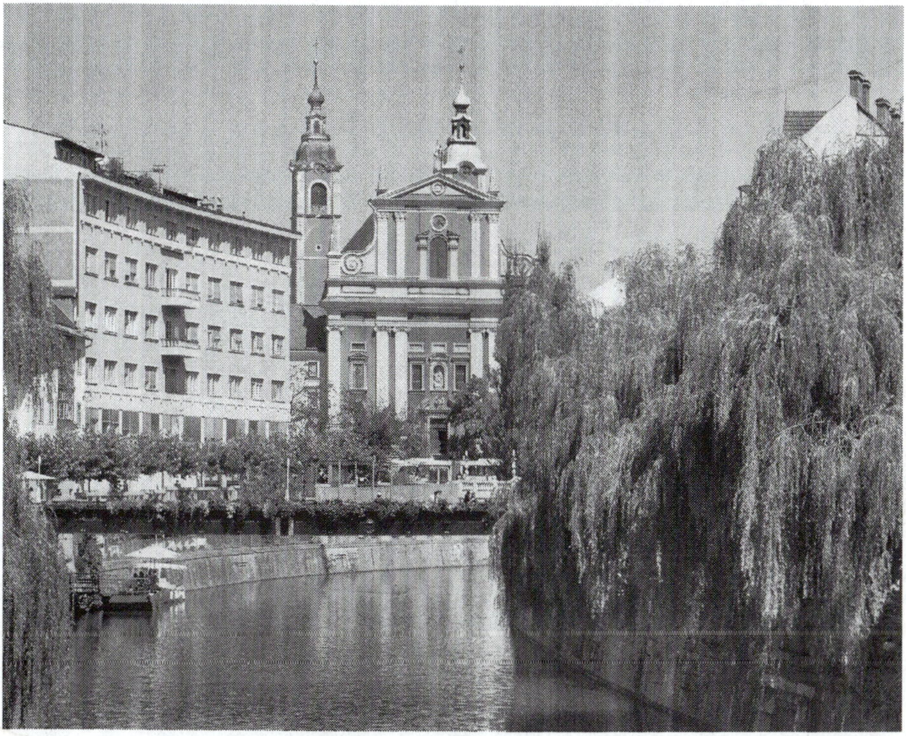

Contents

ZAGREB ... 7
History ... 9
Planning Your Time ... 9
Orientation ... 11

Sights ... 12
Trg bana Jelačića and Kaptol ... 12
- Trg bana Jelačića ... 12
- ☾ Tržnica Dolac ... 13
- Katedrala Marijina Uznesenja ... 14
- Gliptoteka Hazu ... 14
- ☾ Tkalčićeva Street ... 14

Gornji Grad ... 15
- ☾ Kamenita vrata ... 15
- ☾ Muzej grada Zagreba ... 15
- Meštrović Atelier ... 16
- Markov trg ... 16
- Hrvatski povijesni muzej ... 17
- Hrvatski prirodoslovni muzej ... 17
- Hrvatski muzej naivne umjetnosti ... 17
- Jezuitski trg ... 18
- Kula lotrščak ... 18

Donji Grad ... 18
- ☾ Cvjetni trg ... 18
- ☾ Trg maršala Tita ... 18
- Muzej Mimara ... 20
- Etnografski muzej ... 20
- Marulićev trg ... 20
- Botanički vrt ... 20
- Tomislavov trg ... 20
- Strossmayerov trg ... 21
- Zrinjevac ... 21
- Trg žrtava fašizma ... 22

Outside the Center ... 22
- Savska ... 22
- Mirogoj ... 23
- Remete ... 24

Entertainment and Events ... 24
Nightlife ... 24
- Bars ... 24
- Live Music and Dance Clubs ... 25

The Arts ... 25
- Theaters and Dance ... 25
- Opera and Classical Music ... 25
- Film ... 25

Festivals and Events ... 26
- Animafest: World Festival of Animated Films ... 26
- International Folklore Festival ... 26
- Zagreb Summer Festival ... 26
- International Festival of Puppet Theater ... 26
- Zagreb Film Festival ... 26

Shopping ... 26
Antiques and Flea Markets ... 26
Souvenirs ... 26
Food and Wine ... 27
Fashion ... 27
English-Language Bookstores ... 28

Sports and Recreation ... 28
Cycling ... 28
Skiing ... 28
Parks ... 28
- Maksimir ... 28
- Jarun ... 29
- Bundek ... 29
- ☾ Mount Medvednica ... 29

Spectator Sports ... 31
- Soccer ... 31
- Basketball ... 31

Wellness Centers 31

Accommodations 31
Trg bana Jelačića and Kaptol 31
Donji Grad 31
Outside the Center 32

Food 32
Trg bana Jelačića and Kaptol 32
Gornji Grad 33
Donji Grad 34
Outside the Center 36

Information and Services ... 37
Tourist and Travel Information ... 37
Guided Tours 37
Banks and Currency Exchange ... 38
Internet Access and
  Communications 38
Laundry Services 38
Left Luggage 38
Emergency Services 38

Getting There and Around .. 39
Getting There 39
  Air 39
  Train 39
  Bus 39
  Car 39
Getting Around 39
  Tram and Bus 39
  Taxi 40
  Car 40

Around Zagreb 41
Samobor 41
  Sights 41
  Accommodations 42
  Food 42
  Information and Services 42
  Getting There and Around 43
Plešivička Wine Route 43
Zaprešić 43
Marija Bistrica 44

LJUBLJANA 45
History 46
Planning Your Time 47
Orientation 48

Sights 48
Prešernov trg 48
  ◖ Tromostovje 48
East of Prešernov trg 50
  Hiša Eksperimentov 50
  Slovenski Etnografski muzej 50
Vodnikov trg 50
  ◖ Zmajski Most 50
  Glavna tržnica 50
  ◖ Stolnica sveti Nikolaja 51
  Lutkovno Gledališče 51
  ◖ Ljubljanski Grad 51
Old Town 52
  Mestna hiša 52
  Mestni trg 52
  ◖ Gornji trg 52
  Čevljarski Most 53
Left Bank 53
  Slovenska Filharmonija 53
  Moderna galerija 53
  Mestni muzej Ljubljana 53
  Narodna galerija 53
  Narodni muzej 53
  Železniški muzej 53
  Pivovarski muzej 54
  Tobačni muzej 54
Tivoli Park 54

Krakovo 54

Entertainment and Events..55
Nightlife.........................55
  Bars.............................55
  Live Music and Dance Clubs 56
The Arts 57
Festivals and Events 58

Shopping and Recreation....58
Shopping.......................58
  English Books 58
  Food and Wine.....................58
  Souvenirs.........................59
  Antiques..........................59
  Fashion..........................59
  Shopping Centers 59
Sports and Recreation 59
  City Tours........................59
  Recreation 59
  Spectator Sports...................59

Accommodations.............60

Food............................61

Information and Services ...64
Tourist and Travel Information ...64
Banks and Currency Exchange ...64
Internet Access and
  Communications................64
Laundry Services 64
Emergency Services 64

Getting There and Around ..65
Getting There 65
  Air...............................65
  Train.............................65
  Bus..............................66
  Car..............................66
Getting Around...................66
  Bus..............................66
  Car..............................66
  Taxi.............................67
  Bicycle 67

Around Ljubljana 67
Iški Vintgar.....................67
Rakitna.......................67
Zbiljsko jezero..................67
Stična........................67

ZAGREB & LJUBLJANA

ZAGREB

On the surface, Zagreb seems like a modern, bustling city. And in many ways, it is. The streets prowl with luxury cars and designer duds. Large international corporations have attached their logos to shiny new office buildings. And don't be surprised if you hear German, French, or Chinese: Over 45 embassies are located in the rather small capital of approximately 790,000 (closer to one million in the metro area).

Zagreb is the country's business capital, but as you cruise the streets you'll soon realize that much of this business is done over a cup of strong coffee or a long lunch. The cafés are swarmed, particularly on pretty days when it just seems natural to take a meeting outside. At night the socializing continues, from old men in a small bar kicking back a *rakija* (brandy) to young people in a disco pulsing to the latest U.S. dance tunes.

As you delve a little deeper, you'll see a city that changes only what it wants to and at its own pace. At Dolac (Zagreb's main fresh market) the ritual of the daily market remains among the urbanization. Some locals stop for a quick prayer in the Kamenita vrata, just as *zagrebčani* have done for over 250 years, and for the Saturday-morning promenade everyone gets dressed up to see and be seen while they stroll the streets around Cvjetni trg (Flower Square).

Zagreb is perhaps the perfect European capital. With a charming Old Town, a lively café culture, and the requisite cathedral, but without the loads of tourists à la Prague or Vienna, the city is easy to explore in a day before

© SHANN FOUNTAIN ČULO

HIGHLIGHTS

◖ **Tržnica Dolac:** Get into the thick of things, bumping shoulders and bargaining for fresh produce in the city's largest fresh market (page 13).

◖ **Tkalčićeva Street:** This fairy-tale-like street with cafés, restaurants, and local artisans is perfect for strolling, sitting, or window-shopping (page 14).

◖ **Kamenita vrata:** Inside this 13th-century stone gate is an ornate shrine where the faithful pray surrounded by flickering candles (page 15).

◖ **Muzej grada Zagreba:** Zagreb's city museum is well presented and the best way to get a thorough overview of the history and culture of the capital city in just over an hour (page 15).

◖ **Cvjetni trg:** You can't spend time in Zagreb without taking part in the citizens' favorite pastime, a long leisurely coffee (*kava*) on one of the streets near this square while watching the passersby; it's the busiest on a sunny Saturday morning (page 18).

◖ **Trg maršala Tita:** A beautiful square dominated by the wedding cake-like Croatian National Theater, Marshal Tito Square is also home to the must-see Museum of Arts and Crafts, a treasure trove of design and interiors objects in a stunning art nouveau space (page 18).

◖ **Mount Medvednica:** Head to the park's most popular peak, Sljeme, to spend an afternoon on the mountain topped off with a mug of beer and a bowl of steaming *grah* with the locals (page 29).

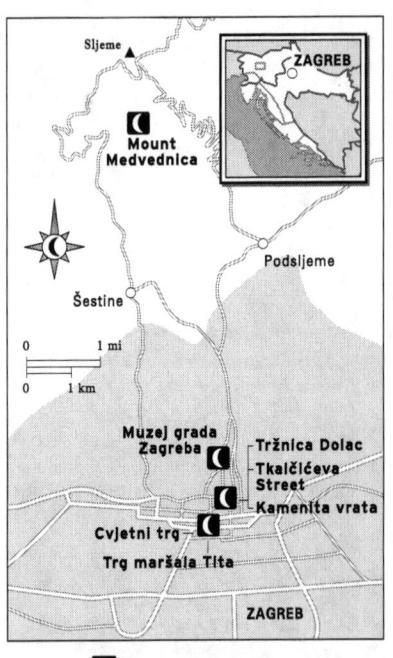

LOOK FOR ◖ TO FIND RECOMMENDED SIGHTS, ACTIVITIES, DINING, AND LODGING.

traveling on to the coast. The museums, while not housing great works of art, are well done and intimate, with exhibits on topics like naive art, local sculpture, and local history. Zagreb boasts glorious Secession architecture, some impeccably restored, some often going unnoticed on decaying gray facades.

Though the city is home to a quarter of Croatia's population, it's easy to get off the beaten path and mix with the locals. The Paris-style parks or the hike up Mt. Sljeme for fresh air, folk music, and great cheap food, are worth staying an extra day for, and several wonderful towns with culture, history, and almost no tourists are easily accessible for a day or even half-day trip.

You'll find the city easy to maneuver. It's not too large and practically everyone under 40 speaks English—often outstandingly good English, better than you'd find in nearby Italy or Germany. The people are friendly, too, and happy to lend a hand or a recommendation.

The city is what you make of it. You can live the glamorous life with the city's high rollers, surrounded by a crowd that's probably dressed better than you are, or share a plate of fried sardines with the locals in a standing-room-only bar. There's the old and the new, and for the most part, it's all good.

Moving west instead of east, Zagreb is changing. It has been changing every year since Croatia's independence. But the core of Zagreb—the buzzing social vibe that moves like honey—remains the same. So whether you spend your time in the museums or in the nightclubs, by far Croatia's best, you can't leave Zagreb without ordering a coffee in a café. Just remember to drink it slowly. It's part of the experience.

HISTORY

In a nutshell, it's amazing that Zagreb has developed into the vibrant town it is today, having been threatened by wars (not to mention some fires and the occasional plague) in almost all nine centuries of its history.

Zagreb is thought to have been settled way back in the Iron Age, but the city wasn't officially established until 1094 when King Ladislaus of Hungary developed a diocese to gain more control over northern Croatia. A settlement called Kaptol developed around the diocese buildings, while Gradec, an area controlled directly by the Hungarian king, sprang up on the neighboring hill.

The two towns fought with each other over land and mills almost from the beginning. On top of that, they had to deal with outside invaders. In a particularly bitter fight with the Mongols in 1242, Gradec was so ravaged that King Bela IV granted Gradec an exemption from jurisdiction, even though he did not exempt them militarily. The exemption, called a "Golden Bull," freed Gradec's citizens of many taxes in order to entice others to move there.

Kaptol wasn't so happy about Gradec's good fortune and escalated the rivalry in 1247 by erecting a tower on Gradec's land; the two communities fought bitterly for decades. Several blows in the 16th century, including the loss of Kaptol lands to the Turks, the defeat of Kaptol by Hapsburg troops, and Gradec's loss of free jurisdiction, diminished the fighting and the two began to be referred to collectively as Zagreb.

Zagreb established itself as the capital of Croatia and Slavonia when the Croatian viceroy Nikola Frankopan moved his headquarters there in 1621. The 17th and 18th centuries were devastating for the city despite its new role as capital. Warfare, several fires, and two bouts of plague almost obliterated Zagreb, with the capital packing up for Varaždin to the north in 1776 and leaving less than 3,000 residents by the end of the 18th century.

The 19th century was the most prosperous for the town. The capital had centered itself in Zagreb once again and, fueled by developing industries, the city added museums, theaters, and schools.

The city continued to thrive until the formation of Yugoslavia in 1918, when the central government moved to Belgrade. And Zagreb underwent a significant transformation in the 1950s and '60s when mayor Većeslav Holjevac built giant apartment complexes across the banks of the Sava River, adding an entire section, called Novi Zagreb (New Zagreb), to the city.

After Croatia's independence in 1991, the city struggled through the war; in the years that followed rampant corruption stagnated the country's growth. Fortunately, the city has finally begun to move forward and is quickly developing into a vibrant capital.

PLANNING YOUR TIME

It only takes a day to get a good overview of Zagreb with a walk through Gornji Grad, visits to a couple of the better galleries and museums, a nice lunch, some window-shopping, and an evening out. If you have two days, though, make sure to spend the second day hiking around Sljeme or visiting one of the cities in the surrounding area, like the sugary little Samobor, on the verge of becoming a suburb of Zagreb.

You'll probably want to use Zagreb as your base for exploring the area; the city's transportation system makes it pretty easy to whiz

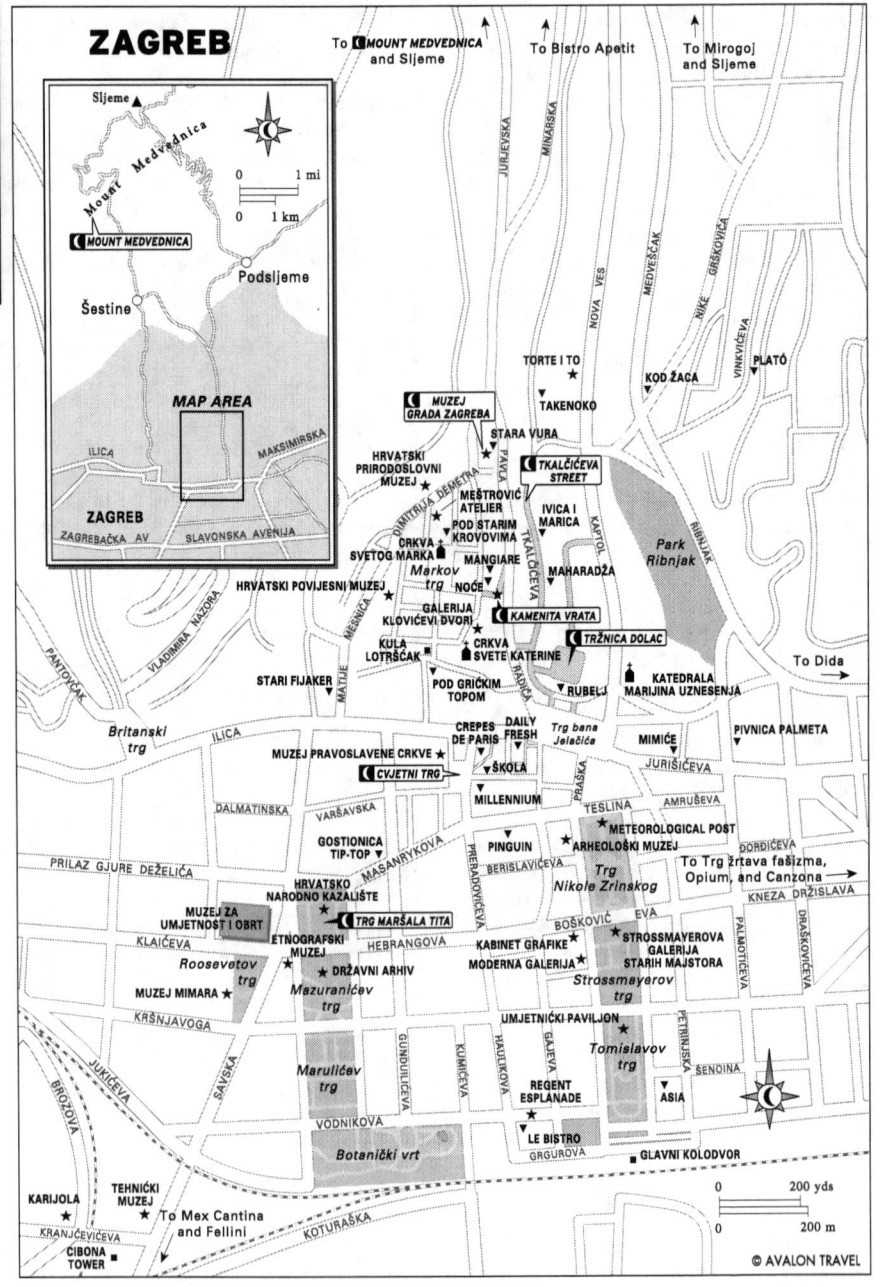

around to most of your stops by tram. If you plan on only spending one day in Zagreb, you'll probably get more for your money at hotels in Samobor (about 30 or 40 minutes by bus from Zagreb's center, depending on the traffic). However, if you don't like traveling on a bus or want to experience some of Zagreb's laid-back nightlife, skip the savings and splurge on a place in town.

Zagreb's main attractions are all within walking distance of each other, though you'll do a lot of walking if you want to traverse both the upper and lower towns in a day. The best plan is to see the highlights and fit in a few other stops that suit your interests, whether that's art or history or shopping, and skip the rest. Architecture buffs might really enjoy making time to see the stunning art nouveau interior at the State Archives.

From September to May, you'll probably find yourself alone in Zagreb's museums, save for the occasional group of schoolchildren. However, tourists are slowly beginning to discover the city, and in summer you'll see the tall flags of tour groups as travelers squeeze in a tour of the old town between their flight and a week on the coast.

Remember that almost everything is closed on Sunday (save for most museums) and most of Gornji Grad's museums are closed Monday. In addition most museums have shortened hours on Saturday and Sunday. Should you find yourself in town on a weekend afternoon, this is the day to head to the slopes of Sljeme or the wide promenades of Maksimir, though on a nice day it may seem the entire city had the same idea.

Winter is usually gray day upon another gray day, though if you happen to end up in town in winter, look on the bright side: You'll have the town's tourist attractions practically to yourself and the city looks quite romantic in winter. Just be sure to grab a bite in the restaurants described as light-filled or sunny. You can also head up to Sljeme, a good choice almost any time of year, for a bit of snow-packed fun.

Spring, early summer, and fall are the best times to visit Zagreb. Though fall can sometimes be rainy, it also gets its share of crisp, sunny days that somehow make the town really shine. Summer is usually bearable, but you may want to avoid town in August, when all the locals are on the coast and the city is empty save yourself and some other tourists traipsing around town.

ORIENTATION

Zagreb can be divided into dozens of neighborhoods, but the two most important for the traveler are Gornji Grad (Upper Town), which comprises the old town and many of the city's most charming attractions, and Donji Grad (Lower Town), rarely referred to as such since it *is* Zagreb—the part of the city where much of the daily hustle and bustle as well as shopping, socializing, and business is carried out. It's also in Donji Grad that you'll find most of the accommodations and restaurants as well as Zagreb's green horseshoe, a network of squares laid out in the 19th century, home to quite a few more important buildings and museums. However, recent development has reduced some of Donji Grad's importance, with business towers being built slightly south of town and Western-style shopping malls popping up in the west toward Samobor and to the south in Novi Zagreb.

Novi Zagreb sprang up in the 1960s, across the Sava River, and is mostly an amalgam of soulless multistory apartment buildings, though the area has come into its own recently with the addition of a new shopping mall and a renovation to the riverside Bundek park, a nice place for a stroll on a sunny day.

However, it's the northern suburbs, toward Sljeme, where the upper middle class live (and the very rich in the Tuškanac area, worth a drive if you're a fan of old houses). The hills, as they are referred to by locals, are bordered on the east by leafy Maksimir park and in the north by Sljeme, a favorite haven of city dwellers on the weekends.

Sights

TRG BANA JELAČIĆA AND KAPTOL

Trg bana Jelačića is the city's main square and a useful base for exploring the town. The **Kaptol** neighborhood that stretches north of the square around the cathedral is filled with restaurants, cafés and shops, culminating in a swank shopping center, Centar Kaptol.

Trg bana Jelačića
Ban Jelačić Square

Trg bana Jelačića has been a meeting point for centuries of locals. Before being officially designated the main square in the 1850s, it served as a point for tax collections and was known as "Harmica" (after the Hungarian *harmincad*, which means a thirtieth).

Today the square is flanked by some beautiful, if not a little over-the-top, examples of classicist and Secessionist architecture sporting ugly signs for multinational corporations on their roofs. What the square lacks in charm it makes up for in convenience. As the city's largest tram stop, it's the perfect departure point for seeing the sights and is a popular meeting place for visitors and locals alike. Before heading off, you can stop at the main **tourist office** (Trg bana Jelačića 11, tel. 01/481-4051, www.zagreb-touristinfo.hr, 8 A.M.–8 P.M. Mon.–Fri., 9 A.M.–6 P.M. Sat.–Sun. June–Sept.; 8:30 A.M.–8 P.M. Mon.–Fri., 10 A.M.–5 P.M. Sat., 10 A.M.–2 P.M. Sun. Oct.–May), located on the southeastern edge of the square.

The square is rimmed with cafés, including the city's legendary **Gradska Kavana**, opened in 1925, long a watering hole for Zagreb's older elite, politicians, and writers, as well as unsuspecting tourists who will find

---

ONE DAY IN ZAGREB

No later than 8:30 A.M., have breakfast at the Regent Esplanade hotel and imagine you're an Orient Express passenger from the era of luxe rail travel. A little before 10 A.M. walk up through the stunning tree-lined **Zrinjevac** to **Trg bana Jelačića,** Zagreb's main square. Follow the row of fresh flower stands topped with red umbrellas and climb the stairs to **Dolac Market** to join the pre-noon crowd bargaining for fresh produce. After you're through with haggling, take a peek at the **Katedrala Marijina Uznesenja** (Cathedral of the Assumption of the Blessed Virgin Mary) and then double back to historical **Tkalčićeva Street** with its petite colorful buildings straight out of a Brothers Grimm tale. The street is crowded with places to stop for lunch, then take a coffee and dessert at **Ivica i Marica** and do a little window-shopping.

From here take the **Stube Bartola Felbingera,** a set of steps marked with a street sign, to the Gornji Grad. Stop for a photo of the colorful roof of **Crkva svetog Marka** (St. Mark's Church) and continue on to visit **Meštrović Atelier** and the **Muzej grada Zagreba** (Zagreb City Museum), adding the **Hrvatski muzej naivne umjetnosti** (Croatian Museum of Naive Art) if you have time. Instead of taking the funicular, take the long way back down by passing through the 13th-century **Kamenita vrata** (Stone Gate).

Have dinner in the lower town, preferably around **Cvjetni trg** (Flower Square), and for dessert stuff your face with gelato at **Millennium** or savor a French-style crepe, locally called *palačinke*, at **Crepes de Paris** – both places are located on or near the square. From here you don't need to look far to find some nightlife. Sip coffee or have a beer with the hundreds of revelers sitting at outdoor cafés along **Bogovićeva.** If the day's history lesson hasn't worn you out, the night is young – at 10 P.M. in Zagreb the party is just getting started.

the prices almost double those of other locations. Trg bana Jelačića is also the site of loud free concerts, political rallies, homecomings for sports figures, and several markets, the largest of which is held at Christmas, with wooden huts selling gifts, souvenirs, and homemade cookies.

Presiding over the square is the **statue of Ban Josip Jelačić,** sculpted by Viennese artist Antun Fernkorn in 1866. Ban Jelačić is a national hero, a Croatian count and general who abolished serfdom and broke ties with Hungary during a rebellion in 1848. The statue used to face north, with Jelačić's saber pointing in rebellion against the Austro-Hungarian empire. The Socialist government dismantled the statue in 1947 and it remained in the Academy of Arts and Sciences until 1990, when it was returned to the square, now facing south, presumably in defiance of its neighbors.

◖ **Tržnica Dolac**
Dolac Market
North of Trg bana Jelačića, Zagreb's main square, follow the row of fresh flower stands topped with red umbrellas and climb the stairs to Tržnica Dolac (until around 2 P.M. daily), the city's main market since 1930. If you're looking for the heart and soul of Zagreb, you'll find it here. Old men drink tiny glasses of brandy at the old cafés along the market's edges and watch the crowd bargaining with the headscarved vendors for fresh produce, herbs, eggs, and homemade cheeses. The atmosphere is warm and friendly and you'll find that even those who can't speak English will try and converse and are always happy to dole out advice and recipes. This is also a great spot to search for souvenirs. From the more predictable embroidered tablecloths, some in good taste and some not, to the quirky elixirs and health remedies, you should be able to find something worth sticking in your suitcase. My recommendation is to buy a fresh *burek* from one of the bread shops on the edge to eat right away, and pick up some local olives or a jar of domestic honey seasoned with lavender or rosemary for the trip home.

Dolac Market, the city's main market

Katedrala Marijina Uznesenja
Cathedral of the Assumption of the Blessed Virgin Mary

The tall, lacy spires of the Katedrala Marijina Uznesenja (Kaptol 31, tel. 01/481-4727, open 7:30 A.M.–7:30 P.M. daily, mass at 7, 8, and 9 A.M. Mon.–Fri. and 7, 8, 9, 10, and 11:30 A.M. Sun., free) can be seen from many parts of Zagreb and though the church is grand, it seems a bit out of place with its more modest surroundings. Built on the site of a small Romanesque church built in 1217 by King Ladislaus, the present cathedral, constructed in the last half of the 13th century, is now a largely neo-Gothic structure. A planned renovation to the cathedral in the 19th century became a near rebuilding of the church after a catastrophic earthquake in 1880. The Viennese architect Hermann Bollé integrated the design of the church, which had suffered from a mish-mash of styles following years of raids, various archbishops, and subsequent renovations that had all left their mark. Four Renaissance choir stalls and a few medieval frescoes are all that remain of the cathedral before the earthquake. Other items of note: the carved panels on the side altar by Albrecht Dürer and a subtle relief by Ivan Meštrović, marking the grave of the controversial Archbishop Alojzije Stepinac. Flanking the southern side of the cathedral, the 18th-century **Archbishop's Palace** is also quite different than the original structure. All that remains today are the medieval-like turrets. Wind around the palace down Vlaška Street and make a left turn where you'll find **Ribnjak** park. Though it's slightly off the beaten tourist track, the sweet little well-maintained park in the heart of the city is a nice spot to eat your finds from Dolac. Once exclusively for the use of Kaptol's priests, the park was opened to the public in 1947.

Gliptoteka Hazu
Glyptotheque of the Croatian Academy of Sciences and Arts

Though this warehouse-like space houses mostly plaster replicas of sculpture and even medieval gravestones, there are a few original pieces, and the whole collection is so well presented that it might be worth the trip if you have some extra time or are in the area. The Gliptoteka Hazu (Medvedgradska 2, tel. 01/468-6050, www.mdc.hr/gliptoteka, 11 A.M.–7 P.M. Tues.–Fri., 10 A.M.–2 P.M. Sat.–Sun., 10Kn) also has exhibits of photography and architecture throughout the year. Check their website or the tourist office to see what's on.

◖ Tkalčićeva Street

Just south of the Gliptoteka in the direction of Trg bana Jelačića, you'll find **Centar Kaptol** (Nova ves 11, tel. 01/486-0241, www.centarkaptol.hr, 9 A.M.–9 P.M. Mon.–Sat.), a shopping mall that houses a multiplex cinema as well as several chic cocktail bars and restaurants frequented by the city's young elite. If you have time, have a slice of cake at local addiction **Torte i to.** As you continue further south, the street runs into Tkalčićeva Street, marked by the beginning of a pedestrian zone. Often

statue of Marija Jurić Zagorka

KRVAVI MOST (BLOODY BRIDGE)

The street called Krvavi Most was once a bridge spanning Medveščak Creek (today Tkalčićeva Street). The creek served as a border between the settlements of Kaptol and Gradec, who rarely got along. Residents from both sides had mills along the creek and often got into skirmishes. However, the bridge really got its name from a 1667 battle in which the soldiers of Viceroy Zrinski attacked the citizens of Gradec, resulting in so many injuries and deaths that the waters of the creek supposedly ran red. The bridge was demolished in 1899 after the creek was filled in, but the tiny street's name keeps a piece of town history alive.

---

referred to simply as Tkalča by the locals, the street is one of the city's social hubs, packed with bars and restaurants.

But what is now a stream of people was once an actual stream bed, forming a boundary between the cities of Gradec and Kaptol. The stream was rerouted due to sewage issues and in the 18th century it became a center for manufacturing, its length lined with workshops making soap, stonework, and liquor, as well as a leather factory.

Today the street's petite colorful buildings with gingerbread windows look like something straight out of a Brothers Grimm tale. However, don't let Tkalčićeva's old world charm deceive you. It is also home to many up-and-coming Croatian artisans. Spend some time shopping the street's jewelry ateliers, galleries, and clothing boutiques.

As you stroll, stop for a photo with the sculpture of **Marija Jurić Zagorka,** one of Croatia's first female journalists and writers.

GORNJI GRAD
Upper Town

Gornji Grad is the heart of Zagreb and the oldest part of town. The area is full of charm and character and has a good portion of the city's best museums and galleries.

◖ Kamenita vrata
Stone Gate

Forming the eastern entrance of the city walls, the cavern-like Kamenita vrata, built in 1241 by the Hungarian King Bela IV, is the only gate that remains of the original four that led into the city. The gate has survived renovations, fires, and various motions by the city to tear it down. The last fire, in 1731, spared a small painting of the Virgin Mary and locals considered it a miracle. A small shrine was formed, with an intricate Baroque iron gate to protect the painting inside a small niche. Candles flicker against the dark space, lit by those who come to pray and seek help from the Virgin of the Stone Gate, whom the archbishop of Zagreb proclaimed a special protector of the city in 1991.

The rooms in the building that line the city gate were originally used as storage areas, but in the 17th century they were converted into small shops. The **pharmacy at Kamenita Street 9** continues the apothecary tradition started in the 14th century, when a pharmacy occupied the same space. A plaque on the building claims that the grandson of the famous author Dante worked in the apothecary in 1399.

◖ Muzej grada Zagreba
Zagreb City Museum

Following the city's development from prehistory to the 20th century, Muzej grada Zagreba (Opatička 20, tel. 01/485-1358, www.mdc.hr/mgz, 10 a.m.–6 p.m. Tues., Wed., and Fri., 10 a.m.–10 p.m. Thurs., 10 a.m.–2 p.m. Sat.–Sun., 10–20Kn) is definitely worth a visit to get a feel for Zagreb's origins and history. Located in the 17th-century convent of the Poor Clares, the museum houses a good mix of exhibits, including portraits, regional dress, everyday objects, socialist posters, and several scale models of Zagreb throughout the centuries. Children will enjoy the re-creations of early 20th-century storefronts and a room dedicated to Croatian animation. Most impressive though is the somber yet exquisite reconstructed portal of the cathedral before its 19th-century renovation.

Just up the street from the museum is **Ilirski trg,** a small square unremarkable save for a café called Palainovka that has a nice gravel terrace and dates from 1846. The area is usually quiet save for occasional bursts of classical music drifting from the windows of the School for Classical Ballet across the street.

Meštrović Atelier
Meštrović Studio

The Meštrović Atelier (Mletačka 8, tel. 01/485-1123, www.mdc.hr/mestrovic, 10 A.M.–6 P.M. Tues.–Fri., 10 A.M.–2 P.M. Sat.–Sun., 20Kn) is in the Zagreb home where Ivan Meštrović lived between 1924 and 1942. This cozy little museum is not only home to some 300 sculptures and drawings by the famous sculptor, but is also an intimate look into the life of the artist. His sunny studio is light-filled even on a rainy day and is so simple and beautiful that it may be hard to leave.

Markov trg
St. Mark's Square

Crkva svetog Marka (St. Mark's Church, Trg svetog Marka 5, tel. 01/485-1611, 11 A.M.–4 P.M. and 5:30–7 P.M. daily, posted hours not always observed, free) just might be one of the most photographed buildings in Croatia. Its colorful roof tiles, the most unique feature of the church, depict the coat of arms of Zagreb (the white castle on a red background) and the Triune Kingdom of Croatia, Slavonia, and Dalmatia (on the left if you're facing the church). You'll probably recognize the red and white checkerboard design, called

---

IVAN MEŠTROVIĆ, CROATIA'S MOST FAMOUS SCULPTOR

The sculptor Ivan Meštrović was born in 1883 in Slavonia, though he spent most of his life in Drniš in Dalmatia. His family was poor and daily chores left no time for him to go to school, though he managed to teach himself to read and write. He was an excellent self-taught artist and managed to land an apprenticeship with a stonemason in Split, where he was discovered and sent to study at Vienna's prestigious Academy of Art.

Meštrović's talent gained him success almost from the start and soon his work was a part of important exhibitions and he was receiving commissions for pieces like *The Well of Life*, in front of the Croatian National Theater. His early pieces reflect the influence of Rodin, whom he knew in Vienna, but his work quickly developed a style all his own.

Meštrović is an important figure not only for his talent as a sculptor but also for the political impact he had as an artist. Committed to the idea of a unified Slav nation, Meštrović began his artistic political statements by including a sculpture of the Serbian hero Kraljević Marko in a 1910 exhibition (today it's in his studio in Zagreb) and placing his work in the Serbian Pavilion at the Rome International Exhibition in 1911 as a statement in support of a unified Slav state.

Meštrović returned to Croatia in the 1920s, turning away from political themes and producing the Račić Memorial Chapel in Cavtat and the statue of Gregorius of Nin for the city of Split.

Imprisoned by the Ustaše in 1941, he was later freed and allowed to leave the country. Although Tito tried to get Meštrović to return to his homeland, the sculptor opted to work as a professor in the United States, where his 1924 sculpture of two Native Americans on horseback decorates Grant Park in Chicago.

Most of the work in his later life revolves around religious themes. He died in 1962 and was laid to rest in the Church of the Holy Redeemer in Otavice, which he had built as his family's resting place years before.

the *šahovnica*, from the modern-day Croatian flag. It has been a symbol of Croatia since medieval times. Dalmatia is represented by the three lions' heads and Slavonia by the animal, actually a marten or *kuna*, the national animal of Croatia and also its currency's namesake.

The Romanesque window on the south side of the church helps support the claim that the church may have been built as early as the 13th century, but earthquake, fire, and well-intentioned reconstructions have left little of the original structure. The simple Gothic church has a rather pretty south portal, original to the church, the work of 14th-century sculptors from Prague.

Outside the church on Markov trg, if you have the feeling you're being watched, you probably are. The square is home to Croatia's government, and men in dark suits protecting the country's politicos are a regular fixture here, explaining the proliferation of sleek black cars parked in the square. At the corner of the square and Cirilometodska Street is the **Town Hall**, now used only for meetings of Zagreb's Town Council. The **Sabor**, or parliament, is housed in the buildings on the eastern side of the square and the **Banski dvor**, the former Baroque residence of the civil governor of Croatia, is now the official seat of the government.

Hrvatski povijesni muzej
Croatian History Museum

Housed in a refreshed Baroque mansion, the small Hrvatski povijesni muzej (Matoševa 9, tel. 01/485-1900, www.hismus.hr, 10 A.M.–6 P.M. Mon.–Fri., 10 A.M.–1 P.M. Sat.–Sun., 10Kn, free Mon.) shows interesting and well-presented temporary exhibitions pulled from the museum's collection of over 140,000 items.

Hrvatski prirodoslovni muzej
Croatian Natural History Museum

The Hrvatski prirodoslovni muzej (Demetrova 1, tel. 01/485-1700, 10 A.M.–5 P.M. Mon.–Fri., 10 A.M.–1 P.M. Sat.–Sun., 15Kn) houses mediocre temporary exhibits, but the most interesting displays are the permanent collections on the 2nd floor. Skeletons, specimens in glass bottles, and stuffed birds and mammals showcased in old-fashioned glass cabinets provide an experience from another era; it's even a little creepy if you happen to be the only visitor. The most amazing display is the 26-foot basking shark, found in the Adriatic in the 1930s.

Hrvatski muzej naivne umjetnosti
Croatian Museum of Naive Art

The small Hrvatski muzej naivne umjetnosti (Sv. Ćirila i Metoda 3, tel. 01/485-1911, www.hmnu.org, 10 A.M.–6 P.M. Tues.–Fri., 10 A.M.–1 P.M. Sat.–Sun., 10Kn) is a don't-miss,

---

NAIVE ART IN CROATIA

The naive art movement in Croatia was started in the late 1920s and 1930s by an academically trained artist, Krsto Hegedušić, who found similarities to French naive painter Henri Rousseau in a small group of painters in the village of Hlebine. With his support, self-taught artists like Ivan Generalić and Franjo Mraz began exhibiting more widely and started using a traditional technique of painting on glass with oil.

Though their work does include a few jaunty pictures of village life, most of Generalić's and Mraz's work is dark and sometimes gruesome, portraying the hardships of peasants and the realities of war. The strong political messages and socialist exhibitions by the Hlebine painters came to an ugly end when Mirko Virius, an artist with a no-holds-barred approach to depicting rural poverty, was killed by the Ustaše in a concentration camp.

The movement then entered a surrealist phase, with works by Ivan Generalić and a new generation of naive painters that included his son Josip and another artist, Ivan Rabuzin, displaying often distorted dreamlike pieces.

Much of naive art today is more decorative than artistic, though the village of Hlebine remains a haven for the purest form of the craft.

if only for the simple, almost organic art it displays. The artists, all untrained, depict sometimes lively, sometimes depressing, scenes of peasant and village life. Most of the works are by the movement's most famous painter, Ivan Generalić, though other artists—even those from outside of Croatia but who embody the naive style—are also on display.

Jezuitski trg
Jesuit's Square

Galerija Klovićevi dvori (Klovićevi dvori Gallery, Jezuitski trg 4, tel. 01/485-2117, www.galerijaklovic.hr, 11 A.M.–7 P.M. Tues.–Sun., 20Kn), once a 17th-century Jesuit monastery, hosts important exhibitions, often of well-known international artists such as Picasso and Chagall. Jezuitski trg, marked by the fountain depicting a fisherman wrestling a snake, spills over into Katarinin trg, where 17th-century **Crkva svete Katerine** (Jesuit Church of St. Catherine, 10 A.M.–1 P.M. daily, free) is a jewel-box Baroque church that is worth a peek. Built between 1620 and 1632, it is the earliest example of Baroque religious architecture in Zagreb.

Kula lotrščak
Burglars' Tower

The Romanesque Kula lotrščak (Strossmayerovo šetalište 9, tel. 01/485-1768, 11 A.M.–8 P.M. Tues.–Sun. May–Oct., call for winter hours, 10Kn), dating from the 13th century, was built by the people of Gradec to protect the city from the Tatars and thieves. At the time, loud bells warned citizens of fires, storms, and the closing of the city gates every evening. In the 19th century a 4th floor was added and later a cannon, to help the churches' bell-ringers know when it was noon.

The cannon is still fired every day at noon, these days letting locals know it's time for lunch. Hike up the narrow staircase for a red-tiled roof view of Zagreb's lower town.

In front of the tower you'll find the **Strossmayerovo šetalište,** or Strossmayer's path, a promenade named after Josip Juraj Strossmayer, bishop of Đakovo. It's worth a stroll to see the magnificent city views.

At the base of Lotrščak tower, the **uspinjača** (funicular, Tomićeva ulica, tel. 01/483-3912, every 10 minutes 6:30 A.M. to 9 P.M. daily, 3Kn one-way) transports passengers—some 750,000 a year—down to the lower town (and back up again if they wish). The 66-meter-long funicular, the shortest in the world, is one of the oldest forms of public transportation in the city, established only one year after the first horse-drawn tram appeared on Zagreb's streets.

DONJI GRAD
Lower Town

Though Donji Grad is slightly younger and a lot busier than the cobblestoned Gornji Grad, the area is a must-see for its museums, its charming network of squares, and most of all, for a taste of bustling Zagreb life. Don't leave without a coffee on Cvjetni trg among the locals.

From the bottom of the funicular that runs from the upper town it's just a short walk south to Ilica, a busy street filled with shops that connects the main square, Trg bana Jelačića, with Britanski trg to the west. Cross over Ilica (watch for trams when you cross) and make your way to Cvjetni trg and the café-lined Bogovićeva for a peek into the social side of the city.

◨ Cvjetni trg
Flower Square

Locals almost never refer to this square by its official name, Preradovićev trg (Preradović's Square), but instead call it Cvjetni trg since it was the site of a Parisian-style flower market until the 1980s, and is still the home of several florist stands. The streets that branch off of the square are the place to be seen on Saturday mornings; sunny days seem to bring out all of Zagreb to the cafés along Bogovićeva and Preradovićeva. Before leaving Cvjetni trg to have a coffee yourself, peep inside the small **Pravoslavna crkva** (Serbian Orthodox Church, hours vary, free). The quiet icon-filled space is a tranquil respite from the activity outside.

◨ Trg maršala Tita
Marshal Tito Square

The **Hrvatsko Narodno Kazalište** (Croatian

TITO SENTIMENT

The tiny village of Kumrovec is all but deserted on a typical day, leaving the birthplace of Josip Broz Tito, his statue in front of the barn, and the rest of the small town rather abandoned and forgotten. But come to town on May 4 (the anniversary of his death) or May 25 (the anniversary of his birthday, long celebrated in former Yugoslavia as Dan Mladosti, or Day of Youth) and you'll see a different story as people gather in the Zagorje village to remember and celebrate Tito. In fact, in 2005, 25 years after Tito's death, there were over 10,000 attendees, from Croatia, Serbia, and Bosnia.

As the years have passed since Tito's death in 1980, the opinion of the former dictator of Yugoslavia has been increasingly positive. Close to half of Slovenians polled in 2000 referred to their opinion of Tito as "excellent" or "good," with only 10 percent responding "poor." There are also plenty of Croatians who remember him fondly, with 60 percent of those polled voting to have his body moved from Belgrade back to Kumrovec (which has not happened, by the way). All this enthusiasm may seem hard to imagine given all of the bad things that went with his regime: The oppression of even a word against Tito, the tendency to throw people into prison over nothing, the Bleiburg massacre, the repression of the Church (state employees were not allowed to attend if they wanted to keep their jobs), and the Croatian Spring debacle are just a few examples.

But people tend to remember the good, such as how Yugoslavians were the wealthiest and freest in Eastern Europe, putting them above their neighbors. Neighbors like Hungary and the Czech Republic have turned the tables on the former Yugoslavia since the fall of the Berlin Wall, and that makes some people nostalgic. Some also miss the security of a state job and a state-provided apartment. Yet plenty remember the hardships of living under the Tito regime. And so for the time being, there will still be one or two news stories a year about people fighting to have the name of Tito Square changed and people fighting to keep it the way it is.

National Theater, Trg maršala Tita 15, tel. 01/482-8532, www.hnk.hr), a massive yellow neo-Baroque wedding cake of a building, dominates the center of the square. Built by Viennese architects Ferdinand Fellner and Herman Helmer, who designed 40 theaters in Europe, the Croatian National Theater was opened in 1895 by the Emperor Franz Josef I, who beat on the balcony above the main entrance with a silver hammer. Inside the domed ceilings, frescoes and gilt-laden balconies are just the right environment for taking in an opera or a ballet, a must if you want to get a peek at the interior. Or, just walk up and see if it happens to be open.

The square is also home to two sculptures, Ivan Meštrović's beautiful 1905 piece *Well of Life*, in front of the theater, and, tucked amongst the trees in the southwestern corner, a piece by Fernkorn of St. George killing a dragon.

On the western side of the square is the **Muzej za umjetnost i obrt** (Museum of Arts and Crafts, Trg maršala Tita 10, tel. 01/488-2111, www.muo.hr, 10 A.M.–1 P.M. Mon., 10 A.M.–8 P.M. Thurs., 10 A.M.–10 P.M. Tues.–Wed. and Fri.–Sun., 20Kn). A veritable wonderland for anyone who loves interiors, its impressive exhibits range from furniture to porcelain to religious art, and the space itself, with its central atrium rimmed with intricate cast-iron handrails, are truly a don't-miss for design fans.

The northern and eastern sides of the square are flanked by the beautiful buildings of Zagreb's **Law Faculty,** holding their own against the theater with their more austere but equally glorious Austro-Hungarian facades. Another of Meštrović's sculptures, *History of the Croats,* stands in front of the yellow building in the northwest corner.

Muzej Mimara
Mimara Museum

Housed in a sprawling 19th-century building, once a local high school, the Muzej Mimara (Trg Franklina Roosevelta 5, tel. 01/482-8100, 10 a.m.–5 p.m. Tues.–Sat., Thurs. until 7 p.m., 10 a.m.–2 p.m. Sun., 40Kn) is the collection of Ante Topić Mimara, who made money abroad and donated the artwork he amassed to the nation. There's lots of controversy surrounding the Mimara, from just who Ante Topić Mimara was, to how he made his money, to whether many of the pieces are real or fake.

With close to 4,000 works of art and some big names attached (no one has ever proved the works are fake, by the way) like Van Gogh, Rubens, Renoir, and Manet, plus prehistoric artifacts, glassware, and sculpture, the museum displays just about everything that falls under the heading "art."

However, unless you're a raging art fan or have never been to a large national museum with famous works of art, you'd probably be better off spending your time visiting places that can only be found in Zagreb, like one of the intimate museums housing local paintings, crafts, or history.

Etnografski muzej
Ethnographic Museum

One of the most under-visited museums in town, the Etnografski muzej (Trg Mažuranića 14, tel. 01/482-6221, www.etnografski-muzej.hr, 10 a.m.–6 p.m. Tues.–Thurs., 10 a.m.–1 p.m. Fri.–Sun., 15Kn, free Thurs.) not only has an impressive collection of regional costumes from around the country, but the building itself, with a gorgeous art nouveau cupola, is worth checking out.

Marulićev trg
Marulić Square

Most people would bypass the **Državni arhiv** (State Archives, Marulićev trg 21, tel. 01/480-1999) on Marulićev trg with only a passing nod to the beautiful building, built in 1913 as the University Library. However, if you have the time it's really worth catching the daily guided tours (noon, 1, and 2 p.m. Mon.–Fri., 20Kn) to see the interior of one of the city's most impressive art nouveau buildings. The building is full of elaborate marble and dripping, decadent crystal chandeliers. Best are the reading rooms, full of soaring ceilings and leaded-glass windows, particularly the Professor's Reading Room. A sort of chapel to academia, the cozy wood-paneled room is filled with its share of opulence, particularly the art nouveau paintings of nudes celebrating higher learning. Behind the building, facing the Botanical Gardens, is a statue of Marko Marulić, the 15th-century poet the square is named after.

Botanički vrt
Botanical Gardens

The land for the Botanički vrt (www.hirc.botanic.hr, 9 a.m.–7 p.m. Tues.–Sun. Apr. 1–Nov. 1, free) was given as a gift to the University of Zagreb from the city in 1889 on the condition that its gates would be open to the public free of charge. Over 100 years later, the university still honors the promise and provides a green oasis for locals and visitors to stop and reflect in the center of the city. Open spring through fall, the winding gravel paths pass through nicely maintained flower beds and hundreds of specimens of trees and shrubs. You'll see families out for a stroll, young couples meeting for a chat during their lunch break, or those who just decided to take a greener detour amid the car-packed city streets. Don't miss the beautifully restored **Exhibition Pavilion,** which as recently as 2004 was decaying into ruin.

Tomislavov trg
Tomislav Square

Continuing east from the Botanical Gardens and passing the grand **Regent Esplanade hotel,** a long stretch of green signals your arrival at Tomislavov trg. In this square named for the first Croatian king a statue of the 10th-century Tomislav on horseback greets travelers spilling out of the **Glavni kolodvor** (Main Train Station). At the other end of the square is the yellow-hued neoclassical **Umjetnički**

REGENT ESPLANADE HOTEL

Even if a night at the Regent Esplanade is out of your budget, this landmark of rail travel deserves a stop to admire the marble and mirrored art nouveau lobby and perhaps have a drink in the piano bar before continuing on your tour of the city.

Built in 1925 for Orient Express passengers when Zagreb was a stop on the original Venice-Simplon Orient Express, the hotel has a long list of famous people who enjoyed its glory days – past guests include Josephine Baker, Charles Lindbergh, Sir Laurence Olivier, and Louis Armstrong.

The hotel has been home to many local scandals since its debut, but the hotel saw its darkest days as the last guests disappeared at the beginning of World War II, only to be replaced by hundreds of German officers when the gestapo chose the hotel as its headquarters in the area. The hotel was neglected during its years as part of Yugoslavia but was tastefully renovated in 2004, regaining the same aura it had so long ago.

---

paviljon (Art Pavilion, Trg kralja Tomislava 22, tel. 01/484-1070, www.umjetnicki-paviljon.hr, 11 A.M.–7 P.M. Mon.–Sat., 10 A.M.–1 P.M. Sun., 20Kn, free Mon.), designed by Viennese architects Ferdinand Fellner and Hermann Helmer. Opened in 1898, it still hosts temporary art exhibits and special functions.

Strossmayerov trg
Strossmayer Square

The **Strossmayerova galerija starih majstora** (Strossmayer Gallery of Old Masters, Trg N. Š. Zrinskog 11, tel. 01/489-5111, www.mdc.hr/strossmayer, 10 A.M.–1 P.M. and 5–7 P.M. Tues., 10 A.M.–1 P.M. Wed.–Sun., 20Kn) is an impressive collection of rich paintings, including works by Tintoretto and El Greco. The most important Croatian work on display is the 11th-century **Bašćanska ploča** (Baška tablet), found on the island of Krk. It is the oldest example of Glagolitic script, the writing of the medieval Croatian church. A statue by Ivan Meštrović of Bishop Juraj Strossmayer, the founder of the Yugoslav Academy for Arts and Sciences, is located behind the building.

Across the street from the Strossmayer Gallery is the **Moderna galerija** (Modern Gallery, Andrije Hebranga 1, tel. 01/492-2371, 10 A.M.–6 P.M. Tues.–Sat., 10 A.M.–1 P.M. Sun., 20Kn), with a nice permanent exhibition entitled *200 Years of Croatian Art*. There are plans to move the museum to Novi Zagreb but work on the building has currently stopped.

Nearby is the **Kabinet grafike** (Graphic Art Gallery, Strossmayerov trg 12, 10 A.M.–6 P.M. Mon.–Sat., admission varies), which holds temporary art exhibitions, some better than others.

Zrinjevac

Possibly the prettiest of Zagreb's squares, lined by giant trees with crackled white and gray bark and surrounded by some of the city's prettiest architecture, Zrinjevac was used as the city's cattle market when it was moved from Trg bana Jelačića in 1830. The square was turned into a park in 1872, the same year the now-massive plane trees were planted, using seeds from Trieste, Italy. It was designed by Milan Lenucij, who went on to design the other squares (Strossmayer, Tomislav, Starčević, Marulić, Mažuranić, Maršal Tito) that form the city's green "horseshoe." Soon Zagreb's elite were constructing mansions along the square; the grand buildings are a great sampling of the city's most prominent architects during the late 19th and early 20th century. In the summer, classical music concerts are often held in the music pavilion and the fountain designed by Bollé still patters with water. However, perhaps the two most interesting features of the square are the **meteorological post,** donated by a local doctor in 1884, where you can check the ever-changing weather, and the **portrait** by Oton Iveković of the square's namesake, Nikola Zrinksi, at No. 20.

While you're there, the **Arheološki muzej** (Archaeological Museum, Trg N. Š. Zrinskog 19, tel. 01/487-3101, www.amz.hr, 10 A.M.–5 P.M. Tues.–Fri., 10 A.M.–1 P.M. Sat.–Sun., 30Kn) is worth a visit. Within an interesting art nouveau building is an impressive collection, from prehistory finds around northern Croatia to the pottery of Greek settlements on the Adriatic coast. The most interesting exhibits are likely the local pottery and jewelry from the Bronze Age, including the famous Vučedol Pigeon, a pouring vessel iconic to the country. There is also an interesting Egyptian exhibit and an exposed mummy, its linen wrappings laden with Etruscan text displayed on the wall beside it. In the summer months, a café serves drinks in the museum's garden.

Trg žrtava fašizma
Victims of Fascism Square

If Zrinjevac is Zagreb's most beautiful square, then Trg žrtava fašizma is its most political. It was christened Trg hrvatskih velikana (Square of Great Croatians) in 1990, but anti-fascist groups protested until the former name was returned. The large circular structure at the square's center, **Dom hrvatskih likovnih umjetnika** (House of Croatian Artists, 11 A.M.–7 P.M. Tues.–Fri., 10 A.M.–2 P.M. Sat.–Sun., admission varies), was completed as an art gallery in 1938, based on a plan by Ivan Meštrović. In 1941 it was turned into a mosque, complete with three minarets, to build Bosnian Muslim support for the NDH, a pro-Nazi puppet state that was in power at the time. In 1945 it became the Museum of People's Liberation; the minarets were pulled down four years later. In 1991 the building was returned to its original purpose and currently houses excellent contemporary art exhibitions.

OUTSIDE THE CENTER
Savska

Though Savska Street is still considered the center by many locals, it's a bit of a trek from the most-frequented sights. If you're at the Mimara Museum, just keep heading south along Savska towards the cylindrical window-filled Cibona

---

NIKOLA TESLA: A GENIUS FOR INVENTION

Nikola Tesla was born in the village of Smiljan, near Lika, in 1856, the son of a Serbian Orthodox priest. He studied in Karlstadt, Graz, and Prague before beginning his career as an electrical engineer in Hungary. He worked in Paris for the Continental Edison Company, then accepted an offer to work for Thomas Edison in New York in 1884.

His letter of introduction to Thomas Edison, written by a Mr. Batchelor, said, "I know two great men – one is you and the other is this young man."

Tesla and Edison later had a falling out. The reasons for the argument are unclear – some say the issue was money and others claim it was an argument of direct current versus alternating current to power long-distance transmission.

Tesla teamed up with financial support from Westinghouse, ultimately winning the battle of the currents and demonstrating the use of alternating current at the Chicago World's Fair in 1893.

Tesla realized many other achievements, such as designing the first hydroelectric power plant at Niagara Falls in 1895 and inventing the Tesla coil, widely used in radio and television sets, in 1891.

He registered over 700 patents worldwide, though much of his genius did not earn him recognition or money, largely because he did not want to reveal his secrets. For instance, Tesla was the father of long-range radio-wave transmissions but did not demonstrate this feat publicly, allowing Guglielmo Marconi to receive credit first (the U.S. patent office later recognized Tesla as the inventor). He also claimed some far-fetched inventions, like a supposed death ray, that caused many to see him as slightly delusional. Yet when Tesla died in 1943 the FBI confiscated his research, leaving his fans to speculate as to what he was really working on.

DRAŽEN PETROVIĆ, BELOVED BASKETBALL STAR

Croatia is a tiny country full of successful athletes, from Wimbledon-winning tennis stars to Olympic gold medalists. But basketball player Dražen Petrović was in a league of his own. Born in Šibenik in 1964, he grew up playing basketball and soon moved from Zagreb's Cibona team to Spain's Real Madrid and finally to the NBA, at a time when European players were the exception rather than the norm. He played for the Portland Trail Blazers and the New Jersey Nets, where he earned the title of team MVP.

In the summer of 1993, after his best NBA season ever, he traveled to Poland to play with the Croatian National Team in a qualification tournament. He made the fateful decision to drive back to Croatia with friends and was killed on the German autobahn in a high-speed crash on June 7, 1993.

The impact his death had on the country was intense. Seeing a wonderful player and a great person struck down in the prime of his life would have been enough cause for sadness. But the death of a role model at a time when young men were still dying for Croatia's independence on the front lines that summer brought the grief to a much deeper level.

The entire nation mourned the death of Dražen Petrović, with over 200,000 people showing up for his funeral. His tomb at Mirogoj is still visited daily by fans who will not forget him.

Tower. Just before reaching Cibona, you'll find the **Tehnički muzej** (Technical Museum, Savska cesta 18, tel. 01/484-4050, www.mdc.hr/tehnicki, 9 A.M.–5 P.M. Tues.–Fri., 9 A.M.–1 P.M. Sat.–Sun., 10Kn), with an interesting array of machinery, engines, a transportation exhibit, and even a WWII submarine. There's also a planetarium and reconstructions of a mine shaft and Nikola Tesla's laboratory. It's worth a stop if you're a big fan of science or have never made it to the Smithsonian. If the above two don't apply to you and you're short on time, feel free to skip this stop.

The rather unattractive **Cibona Tower** marks the home of Zagreb's basketball team, Cibona, which plays next door in the Dražen Petrović Basketball Center. You can also visit the **Dražen Petrović Memorial Center museum** (Trg Dražen Petrović 2, www.drazenpetrovic.net, tel. 01/484-3146, 10 A.M.–5 P.M. Mon.–Fri., 20Kn) for a peek at the life of one of Croatia's most beloved athletes. On display are his jerseys, awards, honors, and photographs that chronicle his rise in basketball.

If you're in the area, make sure to stop at nearby Karijola for one of their excellent pizzas.

Mirogoj

Though it may seem morbid to spend one's holiday poking around a cemetery, Mirogoj (www.gradskagroblja.hr, dawn–dusk daily, free) is not only considered one of the most beautiful memorial parks in Europe, but it is also a major Zagreb landmark. It looks like a fortress for the dead, with its high brick walls topped by cupolas that appear to guard the graves beyond. Known for its grand architecture (the main building was designed by Bollé) and the famous Croatians buried there, it is also interesting for its example of religious tolerance, with Catholic, Orthodox, Muslim, and Jewish tombstones lying side by side. The place is vast—it is the final home of some 300,000 people—but the most outstanding features are found along the arcades that extend from either side of the main building, with their haunting cast-iron lanterns and magnificent, somber sculptures watching over the graves of Croatia's most famous historical figures. To get there from the center take bus #106 from the cathedral or tram #14 going east toward Mihaljevac and get out at the fourth stop (Gupčeva zvijezda) and walk about five minutes uphill.

Remete

Though Remete is quite close to Mirogoj, if you're lacking a navigation system or have a fear of passing giant city buses on curvy roads about the width of a pencil, the best way to get to this leafy suburb of Zagreb by car is to take Bukovačka cesta from Maksimir Park (by bus, hop on #226 from Mirogoj or #203 from Mirogoj's crematorium; ask the driver to alert you to the stop for Remetska crkva) and follow it to the top of the hill. As you begin your descent, you'll see **Crkva svete Marije** (Church of St. Mary, tel. 01/450-0500, generally open dawn–dusk daily, free), a Gothic structure with a salmon and white Baroque facade. The church is swamped with the faithful on Marian feast days, particularly August 15 (Assumption, locally known as Velika Gospa). The interior of the church is stunning in an eclectic way, with an over-the-top marble altar, whose 15th-century wooden statue of the Madonna is said by many to bestow miracles. But the most beautiful feature of the church is the delicate, fading frescoes by Ivan Ranger, the famed monk whose artwork graces many north Croatian churches.

Entertainment and Events

NIGHTLIFE
Bars

The over-20 set can easily start a bar-hopping tour of the city around Bogovićeva. The nearby **Maraschino** (Margaretska 1, tel. 01/481-2612, 7 A.M.–1 A.M. Sun.–Thurs., 7 A.M.–4 A.M. Fri.–Sat.) is a good place to start; its tables are jammed with a young professional crowd from weekday mornings to weekend nights when the bar amps it up with DJ music. **Bulldog** (Bogovićeva 6, tel. 01/481-7393, 8 A.M.–11 P.M. daily) is a pub around the corner with lots of outdoor seating and a pretty impressive wine selection from its sister bar, **Bulldog XL** (same location, same times). Just down the street, slightly hidden **Škola** (Bogovićeva 7/2, tel. 01/482-8196, www.skolaloungebar.com, 10 A.M.–1 A.M. Mon.–Sat., 11 A.M.–midnight Sun.) fills up its gallery-like space with the beautiful people after dark.

Zagreb has several lounge bars with comfy chaises from which to strike a pose. The most popular downtown spots are the ultrachic **Khala** (Nova Ves 11, tel. 091/321-1338, 8 A.M.–1 A.M. Sun.–Thurs., 8 A.M.–3 A.M. Fri.–Sat.), which also functions as a wine bar, in Centar Kaptol, and **Hemingway** (Trg maršala Tita 1, tel. 098/980-5000, www.hemingway.hr, 7 A.M.–3 A.M. daily), a lounge bar opposite the HNK (Croatian National Theater). Further afield, **People's** (Hektorovićeva 2, tel. 01/604-0521, www.peoples.hr, noon–1 A.M. Sun.–Wed., noon–3 A.M. Thurs.–Sat.) and **Spoon** (Slavnoska avenija 6, tel. 01/631-0860, www.spoon.hr, 10 A.M.–2 A.M. daily) cater to plenty of in-crowd primp and show. Keep in mind that some of these spots don't get going until at least 11 P.M.

Thirtysomethings who like to pretend they're in their twenties will enjoy **Movie Pub** (Savska 141, tel. 01/605-5045, www.the-movie-pub.com, 7 A.M.–2 A.M. Mon.–Wed., 7 A.M.–3 A.M. Thurs., 7 A.M.–4 A.M. Fri.–Sat., 6 P.M.–2 A.M. Sun.), with lots of beers on tap in a huge space that manages to fill up on weekends and karaoke on Wednesday and Thursday. Literary types should try **Sedmica** (Kačićeva 7A, 7 A.M.–11 P.M. daily), where the patrons, instead of the decor, give the bar an artsy vibe.

Students might want to try **Spunk** (Hrvatske bratske zajednice, tel. 01/615-1528, 7 A.M.–midnight Mon.–Sat., 6 P.M.–midnight Sun.), outside the National University Library, which doesn't look that promising but is still filled with laid-back people and good music with occasional live bands. **Krivi put** (Runjaninova 3, no phone, hours vary), whose name means "wrong way," is a smoky college bar with cheap drinks and a terrace for summer swilling. For something edgier (at least in Zagreb terms),

ENTERTAINMENT AND EVENTS

Dobar Zvuk (Gajeva 18, tel. 01/487-2222, noon–11 P.M. Mon.–Sat.) is a serious rocker bar that doesn't take itself too seriously.

Live Music and Dance Clubs

Close to the center, **Gjuro II** (Medveščak 2, tel. 01/468-3367, www.gjuro2.hr, 9 P.M.–2 A.M. daily) has a small dance floor, theme nights, and a crowd that grows younger as the week goes on. **Kset** (Unska 3, tel. 01/612-9758, www.kset.org, 9 A.M.–3 A.M. Mon.–Fri., 10 P.M.–3 A.M. Sat.) has a cult-like following for its great jazz and DJ mixing. It's popular with students and a slightly alternative older crowd.

Fans of jazz will like **B.P. Club** (Nikole Tesle 7, tel. 01/481-4444, www.bpclub.hr, 10 A.M.–2 A.M. daily) or **Sax!** (Palmotićeva 22, tel. 01/487-2836, www.sax-zg.hr, 9 A.M.–4 A.M. daily); Sax! hosts blues and rock bands as well. Both places have a good drinks menu and lots of places to sit if you're not into shaking your thing. **Tvornica** (Pavla Šubića 2, tel. 01/777-8673, www.tvornica-kulture.hr, 9 A.M.–10 P.M. Mon.–Fri., 10 P.M.–4 A.M. Sat. and during events) is a quirky club in a large space near the bus station. The entertainment varies widely from gypsy tunes to rock to fashion shows, but the bands are usually high quality. Call or check the website to find out what's on before heading out. For really late nights, head to **Ritz Cabaret** (Petrinjska 4, tel. 099/660-7182, 10 P.M.–6 A.M. Wed.–Sat.). Full of luxe vibe, it caters to a thirty-something, slightly flashier crowd with VIP tables available by reservation.

If you're in the mood for some club hopping, make a beeline to Jarun, where **Aquarius** (Matija Ljubeka bb, Jarun, tel. 01/364-0321, www.aquarius.hr, 9 A.M.–6 A.M. Thurs.–Sat.) brings in big-name DJs and local stars and **Piranha Bar** (Jarunska obala, tel. 091/462-9234, www.piranha.com.hr, 8 A.M.–2 A.M. Wed.–Thurs., 8 A.M.–4 A.M. Fri.–Sat., 8 A.M.–midnight Sun.–Tues.) swarms with well-dressed kids.

Closer to the center, **Boogaloo** (Ulica Grada Vukovara 68, tel. 01/631-3021, www.boogaloo.hr, 8 P.M.–4 A.M. Tues.–Sun.) is an all-purpose dance club with popular tunes and salsa nights. And if your feet need a break from boogying, Boogaloo has a lounge room with comfy couches and a bar for refreshments.

THE ARTS
Theaters and Dance

Break out the opera glasses at **Hrvatsko Narodno Kazalište** (Croatian National Theater, Trg maršala Tita 15, tel. 01/482-8532, www.hnk.hr, box office 10 A.M.–7:30 P.M. Mon.–Fri., 10 A.M.–1 P.M. Sat. and 1.5 hours before performances), also known as **HNK,** where drama and ballet are staged in a beautiful gilt and frescoed atmosphere. **Exit** (Ilica 208, tel. 01/370-4120, box office 4:30–8 P.M. Tues.–Sat.) is a small studio theater with some good contemporary plays. Both theaters stage performances almost exclusively in Croatian.

Opera and Classical Music

The **HNK** (Croatian National Theater, Trg maršala Tita 15, tel. 01/482-8532, www.hnk.hr, box office 10 A.M.–7:30 P.M. Mon.–Fri., 10 A.M.–1 P.M. Sat. and 1.5 hours before performances) has opera performances, while **Koncertna dvorana Vatroslav Lisinski** (Vatroslav Lisinski Concert Hall, Trg Stjepana Radića 4, tel. 01/612-1167, www.lisinski.hr, call or go online for a list of concerts) brings in big names like Cesaria Evora on occasion as well as regular performances by the Zagreb Philharmonic and the Croatian Radio Symphony Orchestra.

Film

The best thing about seeing a movie in Croatia is that they are all in the original language, save for some animated features, with Croatian subtitles. Zagreb has three big multiplexes but the two located closest to the center are **Continental Movieplex** (Nova Ves 17, Centar Kaptol, tel. 01/486-0777, www.movieplex.hr), at the end of Tkalčićeva in Centar Kaptol, and **Cinestar** (Branimirova 29, tel. 01/468-6600, www.blitz-cinestar.hr), in Branimir Centar near the Sheraton. You can often catch a show in town at the old **Europa** (Varšavska 3, tel. 01/487-2888, www.kino europa.hr) on Cvjetni trg, which screens mostly art-house films.

FESTIVALS AND EVENTS

Animafest: World Festival of Animated Films

This 30-year-old festival, now held on a yearly basis, screens excellent feature-length and short animated films from international filmmakers, including categories for student films and short films made for the Internet (late May–early June, www.animafest.hr).

International Folklore Festival

Teeming with colorful costumes from all over Croatia, Trg bana Jelačića comes alive with dance and music performances and stands selling hundreds of handicrafts during the International Folklore Festival (last weekend in July, www.msf.hr).

Zagreb Summer Festival

Though much of Zagreb empties out during summer, the Zagreb Summer Festival (mid-July–mid-Aug.), featuring orchestral and chamber music, still plays to good-sized crowds who come to enjoy the wide range of international performers.

International Festival of Puppet Theater

Featuring wonderful puppet productions from all over central and eastern Europe, the International Festival of Puppet Theater (late Aug.) is a must-see for kids, and has a few shows aimed at adults as well.

Zagreb Film Festival

A relatively new film festival that is already gaining in importance, the Zagreb Film Festival (Oct., www.zagrebfilmfestival.com) screens some 70 films from around the world in three Zagreb cinemas.

Shopping

ANTIQUES AND FLEA MARKETS

Hit **Britanski trg**'s antiques market (8 A.M.–2 P.M. Sun.) for old postcards from the region, interesting jewelry, and various knickknacks from another era. You'll find some of the same things for less than half the price at **Hrelić** (Sunday morning, pros arrive at 7 A.M. or earlier), the city's flea market in Novi Zagreb, fittingly located near the trash dump where three quarters of the stuff should have gone before it was fished out for sale by the vendors. However, if you're willing to peruse the items on blankets strewn about the ground, you'll probably find something worth taking home. Common finds are intricately carved brass Turkish coffee grinders and long wooden bowls used for kneading dough.

SOUVENIRS

Though some items are a bit overpriced, **Bakina kuća** (Strossmayerov trg 7, tel. 01/384-3805, www.bakina-kuca.hr, 8 A.M.–9 P.M. Mon.–Fri., 9 A.M.–5 P.M. Sat.) is a one-stop shop for sweets, *rakija,* souvenirs, and herb-based cosmetics.

For a practical item that will also remind you of your trip to Zagreb, **Cerovečki Kišobrani** (Ilica 49, tel. 01/484-7417, www.kisobrani-cerovecki.hr, 8:30 A.M.–8 P.M. Mon.–Fri., 8:30 A.M.–3 P.M. Sat.) sells the same red handmade Šestine umbrellas that cover Dolac market stands.

Dolac itself is a spot to pick up embroidered tablecloths and other handicrafts in the stalls at the back of the market, near the fish section and up the stairs.

For kids, **Hlapićev dućan** (Katančićeva 3, tel. 01/481-7224, www.hlapic.net, 9 A.M.–7:30 P.M. Mon.–Fri., 9 A.M.–5 P.M. Sat., also in Centar Kaptol shopping center) stocks toys and knickknacks from the well-loved Croatian book character Hlapić, created by author Ivana Brlić Mažuranić.

FOOD AND WINE

There are lots of places to get your gourmet on in Zagreb. Among the best are **Pršut Galerija** (Vlaška 7, tel. 01/481-6129, 9 A.M.–8 P.M. Mon.–Fri., 9 A.M.–2 P.M. Sat.), selling all sorts of home-cured ham, similar to Serrano ham, and **Vinoteka Bornstein** (Kaptol 19, www.bornstein.hr, 9 A.M.–7 P.M. Mon.–Fri., 2–7 P.M. Sat.), a great wine shop in a dark Kaptol (the neighborhood, not the mall) cellar, with a strong showing of Croatian wines. The owners are also local emissaries for all things Istrian and are a great source of info if you're headed that way.

Franja (Vlaška 62, tel. 01/455-6391, www.franja.hr, 7 A.M.–8:30 P.M. Mon.–Fri., 7 A.M.–5 P.M. Sat.) sells the local Franck brand of coffees, and while real coffee connoisseurs will not be impressed, it makes a decent souvenir.

If you're dying for real tea, which is a rare find in Croatia, stop by **Kuća Zelenog Čaja** (Ilica 14, tel. 01/483-0667, www.kuca zelenogcaja.com, 9 A.M.–8 P.M. Mon.–Fri., 9 A.M.–3 P.M. Sat.) for a good selection of loose-leaf tea.

FASHION

Since the tie was actually invented by Croats, a necktie is a nice souvenir from the country. **Croata** (Ilica 5—inside the Oktogon, tel. 01/481-2726, www.croata.hr, 8 A.M.–8 P.M. Mon.–Fri., 8 A.M.–3 P.M. Sat.), Croatia's "official" tie store, has a good selection and purchases are packaged with a little history of the cravat.

Zagreb is the home of some interesting and unique fashion design. A couple of stores to check out are **Boudoir** (Radićeva 25, tel. 01/481-3464, www.boudoir.hr, 1–8 P.M. Mon.–Fri., 9 A.M.–3 P.M. Sat.) and **Stolnik** (Vlaška 58, tel. 01/461-7000, www.moda-stolnik.com, 9 A.M.–8 P.M. Mon.–Fri., 9 A.M.–3 P.M. Sat.). For jewelry, head to Tkalčićeva, where **Lazer Rok Lumezi** (Tkalčićeva 53, tel. 01/481-4030, www.nakit-lumezi.hr, 10 A.M.–8 P.M. Mon.–Fri., 10 A.M.–3 P.M. Sun.) designs unique pieces that will surely get you noticed. If you're

shopping for bargains at Dolac Market

not looking for wearable art so much as some fun jewelry to take home to friends, **Lapis** (Tkalčićeva 32, tel. 01/481-0255, 10 A.M.–6 P.M. Mon.–Fri., 10 A.M.–2 P.M. Sat.) has colorful, wiggly pieces that make great presents.

ENGLISH-LANGUAGE BOOKSTORES

Algoritam (Gajeva 1, tel. 01/481-8672, www.algoritam.hr, 8:30 A.M.–9 P.M. Mon.–Fri., 8:30 A.M.–3 P.M. Sat.) has several stores throughout Zagreb, but the main location at Gajeva near Trg bana Jelačića has the best selection of books, DVDs, and computer games. They also carry a range of foreign newspapers and weekly magazines, though sometimes a day or two behind (or a week or two in the case of gossip rags), if you're itching to read the *New York Times*. If Algoritam doesn't have what you're looking for, **Profil Megastore** (Bogovićeva 7, tel. 01/487-7300, www.megastore-profil.hr, 9 A.M.–10 P.M. Mon.–Sat.) is just a short walk away and has an in-store café and a large selection of stationery supplies. If you're traveling around Europe, it's worth checking out the English bookstores in Zagreb as they offer an even better selection than you'll find in large cities like Frankfurt.

Sports and Recreation

CYCLING

Cycling on Zagreb's city streets, particularly on weekdays, is not recommended. Though the city has installed some designated bike lanes in the past few years, you'll usually find quite a few cars parked along them and drivers aren't used to sharing the narrow roads with cyclists. If you'd like to bike in parks like Maksimir and Jarun, you can rent a bicycle from the **Fumić Bicycle Shop** (in Jarun near *ulaz petrine*—Petrina entrance, tel. 01/466-4233, www.fumic-bicikli.hr) for 80Kn per day or 20Kn per hour. Mr. Fumić also organizes bike rides from his shop in Jarun, starting at 9 A.M. on good-weather Sundays. Rides traverse the surroundings of Zagreb and are 80 to 120 kilometers long.

SKIING

Sljeme has decent skiing for beginners or for those that just want to keep their skills from getting too rusty. During the ski season more info can be found by calling 01/455-5827 and online at www.sljeme.hr. Local outfitter **Sport4You** (Ilica 213, tel. 01/377-0150, www.sport4you.hr, 9 A.M.–5 P.M. Mon.–Fri., daily equipment rental approx. 140Kn) offers ski lessons (with English-speaking instructors) and equipment rental on Sljeme. Call ahead to make arrangements.

PARKS
Maksimir

While it may not be a must-see, Maksimir (tram nos. 11 or 12, direction Dubrava, dawn–sunset daily) should make the top of your list if you have any extra time in Zagreb for a leisurely stroll. Located about a five-minute drive east of Trg bana Jelačića, the park was founded in 1774 by the Bishop Maximilian Vrhovac and was originally constructed in the Baroque French style, with three radial paths that still exist today. Subsequent Bishops Aleksandar Alagović and Juraj Haulik expanded on his design, incorporating many English features. Despite its wide, straight promenade, there are dozens of smaller forested paths where you can lose an afternoon. The park is also home to the small but well-thought-out **Zagreb Zoo** (tel. 01/230-2198, www.zoo.hr, 9 A.M.–8 P.M. daily May–Sept., 9 A.M.–4 P.M. daily Oct.–Apr., 20Kn), and children will appreciate the **Echo Pavilion,** built in 1840, located near the zoo's entrance. When you're done with exercise, join a crowd of locals at the **Gazebo** (no phone, hours vary), rising above the end of the main promenade, for a peaceful view of the park and a little liquid refreshment.

Jarun

A 15-minute drive west from the center (direction Samobor) will take you to Jarun (tel. 01/303-1888, www.jarun.hr, from Trg bana Jelačića take tram #17 to Jarun), a popular spot for *zagrebčani* to while away a weekend afternoon. With two lakes and six different islands, the 585-acre park complex, built for the 1987 University Games, has a variety of recreational and water sports available. There is also a nice network of flat paths, perfect for in-line skating (rent by the hour from the Fumić Bicycle Shop, described earlier) or biking around the lakes. For those who like to fish, the lake is well stocked and a daily fishing license is available. But Jarun is perhaps best known as a nightlife destination for Zagreb's younger crowd, with a strip of bars and clubs lining the lakeshores—perfect for party-hopping types.

Bundek

A lake just off the banks of the Sava River in Novi Zagreb, Bundek (from Trg bana Jelačića take tram nos. 14 or 6, direction Novi Zagreb, to stop Sopot, from there a short walk) experienced a rebirth in 2006. The area, once ridden with unsavory types lurking about and the litter they left, is now a clean, busy, family-friendly park with impeccably maintained flower beds, great paths, one of the nicest playgrounds in Zagreb, and a pebbly beach serviced by a few waterside cafés. If it's a hot day, it's a pleasant place to take a dip.

◖ Mount Medvednica

With its densely forested slopes and endless trails, an excursion to the Mount Medvednica range is great almost any time of the year. The range stretches along the northern side of town, from the western suburbs to slightly east of the center; its highest peak and most developed mountain, **Sljeme,** is reached by driving along Ribnjak out of the center until you see signs pointing right to Sljeme via Gračanska cesta. By tram, take #14 to Mihaljevac and then #15 to the last stop at Dolje. From there it's a short 10-minute walk to the cable car station (*žičara*,

Sljeme, a popular outing from Zagreb

A DAY ON SLJEME

Winding your way up Mount Sljeme on a fall day, leaves trickle onto the pavement as you pass hikers and cyclists all basking in the flickering light that filters through the forest of beech. Fall – or any other time of year for that matter – is perfect for enjoying one of Zagreb's traditional weekend outings. Since the 19th century, *purgeri* (the local name for people from Zagreb) have been visiting the mountain for rest and relaxation.

You can choose the easiest way to climb towards the summit of the highest peak of the Medvenica mountain range – a car. For those more athletically inclined, the steep hike or bike ride will still challenge your hamstrings. And if you're not afraid of heights, the cable car offers panoramic views of the golden treetops.

It is difficult to imagine you're only minutes from the city center, with its crowded cafés filled with designer-clad individuals wielding the latest models of mobile phones. Here you can enjoy a moment's quiet reflection, appreciate the local flora and fauna, and take a time out from the busyness of city life.

However, the most charming attractions of Sljeme are the many stops where you can replenish your reserves for the return journey. Many of these alpine-style huts, with names like Želježnički Dom (Railway Home) or Dom Grafičar (Home Grafičar), were built by state-run companies during communism for their workers to enjoy. My favorite place to visit is **Puntijarka** (9 A.M.-7 P.M. daily except major holidays), the restaurant of the Mountaineering Society. Old and young gather to share bowls of beans (locally called *grah*) and mugs of beer at dozens of picnic tables outfitted with holes to accommodate walking sticks. The lively sounds of the musicians' accordion and *tambura* accompany the crowd's appetite. Beginning outside, a long line forms to sample simple but enchanting entrées including roast chicken, sausages, and walnut cake.

On a crisp day you'll see young and old, biking enthusiasts sharing tables with children in strollers, though it's the established set that draws the most attention. Old men with coordinating scarves, alpine hats, and pants similar to jodhpurs are out in large groups – yes they take their hiking seriously. Feel free to sit down at any table with a free spot and start a conversation over some mulled wine.

For those desiring to experience times past, an outing to a place like Puntijarka is certainly not to be missed. The spirit of community and equality that enthuses the cool air today is a stark contrast to the new Eastern Europe, where the middle class is a minority. In some ways it reminds one of the intriguing and romantic Croatia at the beginning of its independence. Gone are the threadbare art deco booths of Zagreb's Theater Café and the communist white shoes of its waitresses. The blue trams that once circled the town in uniformity now zip past advertising movies and soft drinks. Gray, crackling facades are being colorfully restored one by one to their Austro-Hungarian glory. Many things are changing, most for the better, in the new, more Western Croatia. Yet this sense of society, of the communing of the people, may be one remnant of the old regime worth preserving.

---

8 A.M.–8 P.M. on the hour daily, 11Kn one-way, 17Kn round-trip) or about a three-hour trek to the top. In nice weather, a hike or an outdoor lunch near the top are reasons enough to go. In snowy weather, there are some bunny slopes and spots for sledding to keep you occupied.

Four kilometers southwest of Sljeme is the 13th-century **Medvedgrad** fortress. Built to defend against Tatar attacks, it was abandoned in 1571 and remained neglected until it was rebuilt in the 1990s. An **Oltar domovine** (Homeland Altar) with an eternal flame surrounded by sculptures in the form of tears looks somewhat out of place in its medieval surroundings, though it's an important photo stop for Croatian politicians. There are some great views from here and a restaurant serving typical dishes. From Sljeme, follow the marked paths from the Tomislavov dom hotel or take about an hour's walk from Šeštine church.

SPECTATOR SPORTS
Soccer
The **Maksimir stadium** (Maksimirska 128, tel. 01/484-3769) across from Maksimir Park is home to games of the Croatian National Team and the local Dinamo, whose fans deck out in the team's signature blue for loud and exciting matches. The main season is August to May (with a break in January and February) and tickets run a cheap average of 30Kn and can be purchased from kiosks near the entrance.

Basketball
Cibona draws pretty decent-sized crowds to watch quality basketball at the **Dražen Petrović Basketball Center** (Savska cesta 30, tel. 01/484-3333, around 30Kn at the door) from September through April.

WELLNESS CENTERS
Zagreb is full of spas and wellness centers, though none offer out-of-the-ordinary services. **Wellness Centar Coner** (Trpimirova 2, tel. 01/539-0555, www.coner.hr, 6:30 A.M.–10:30 P.M. Mon.–Sat., 9 A.M.–10:30 P.M. Sun.), in the Sheraton, offers a full range of massages, facials, and pedicures as well as an indoor pool, fitness center, and sauna. Just across from Centar Kaptol are some of the best facials in the city at **Murad** (Medvedgradska 1C, tel. 01/466-6473, call for hours), run by a doctor of dermatology.

Accommodations

Some of the cheapest accommodation can be found by staying in a private home or renting a short-term apartment. Several companies offer these sorts of accommodation, starting from 150Kn; try **NEST** (Boškovićeva 7A, tel. 01/487-3225, nest@nest.hr, www.nest.hr), **InZagreb** (Remetinečka 13, tel. 091/652-3201, info@inzagreb.com, www.inzagreb.com), or **Evistas** (Augusta Šenoe 28, tel. 01/483-9554, evistas@zg.t-com.hr, www.evistas.hr).

Since Gornji Grad is currently devoid of formal accommodations, you'll need to sift through these agency's offerings to find rooms or apartments located in the oldest part of Zagreb. Be aware that not all of these apartments have air-conditioning—definitely a consideration in the height of summer. Otherwise, hotels and hostels are found in the lower part of town, with most being quite expensive for what you get in return.

TRG BANA JELAČIĆA AND KAPTOL
Under 700Kn
The **Fulir Hostel** (Radićeva 3A, tel. 01/483-0882, fulir@fulir-hostel.com, www.fulir-hostel.com, 139Kn per person) opened in 2006, just off Trg bana Jelačića in a quiet location with multi-bed rooms.

700–1,400Kn
Though the rooms are a bit worn, the location of **Hotel Dubrovnik** (Gajeva 1, tel. 01/487-3555, reservations@hotel-dubrovnik.hr, www.hotel-dubrovnik.hr, 1,066Kn d., including breakfast) can't be beat. It's right on Trg bana Jelačića and has a friendly staff and a decent buffet breakfast.

DONJI GRAD
Under 700Kn
If you don't mind staying in a private home, **Ilički Plac Private Accommodation** (Britanski trg 1, tel. 098/419-231, ilicki@email.t-com.hr, www.ilicki.com, 426Kn d.) is a great value, with the added bonus of getting a feel for living in one of the center's high-ceilinged apartments. It's also conveniently located on Britanski trg for fans of Sunday-morning antiques-hunting.

Billed as Zagreb's first design hotel, the

modern **Arcotel** (Branimirova 29, tel. 01/469-6000, allegro@arcotel.at, www.arcotel.at, 575Kn d.) is slightly out of the way, but has good jazz in the lobby bar two nights a week. The **Best Western Hotel Astoria** (Petrinjska 71, tel. 01/480-8900, info@hotelastoria.hr, www.bestwestern.com, 568Kn d., including breakfast) is a fairly new hotel in a convenient location to the tram station and within a 10-minute walk of Trg bana Jelačića.

700-1,400Kn

The historic **Palace** (Strossmayerov trg 10, tel. 01/489-9600, palace@palace.hr, www.palace.hr, 1,024Kn d., including breakfast) has Secession charm, in particular the art nouveau lobby, and a super location—however ask for a renovated room if you want to get your money's worth.

Though the comfy **Sheraton** (Kneza Borne 2, tel. 01/455-3535, www.sheraton.com, 1,150Kn d., including breakfast) is a favorite with the business set and has a great spa and decent indoor pool, if you're looking for luxury, skip it (it's out of the way for the price and notorious with taxi drivers looking to rip up unsuspecting foreigners).

Instead, stay in the ❰ **Regent Esplanade** (Mihanovićeva 1, tel. 01/456-6666, info.zagreb@rezidorregent.com, www.regenthotels.com, 1,074Kn d., including breakfast), built for Orient Express passengers in 1925 and fastidiously renovated.

OUTSIDE THE CENTER
Under 700Kn

The **Hostel Lika** (Pašmanska 17, tel. 01/618-5375, info@hostel-lika.com, www.hostel-lika.com, 96Kn per person) looks depressing from the outside but consistently gets good reviews from backpackers.

The **Ravnice Youth Hostel** (Ravnice 38D, tel. 01/233-2325, www.ravnice-youth-hostel.hr, 121Kn per person), near Maksimir Park, is a bit more secluded but a slightly more upscale version of the traditional hostel.

Leave the center to find the best deals on accommodation. The **Hotel Fala** (Trnjanske ledine 18, tel. 01/611-1062, hotel-fala@hotel-fala.zg.hr, www.hotel-fala.zg.hr, 476Kn d., including breakfast) has basic but clean rooms about a half-hour walk from the center.

Food

TRG BANA JELAČIĆA AND KAPTOL
Cafés and Desserts

❰ **Torte i to** (Nova Ves 11, tel. 01/486-0691, www.torte-i-to.hr, 9 A.M.–11 P.M. daily, 25Kn) is a bit hard to find, tucked in the back of the 1st floor of Centar Kaptol shopping mall, but it's worth the effort to sample the best cakes in Zagreb. *Torta ledeni vjetar* (cold wind cake) is the unofficial house specialty, though the cheesecake is stupendous too.

Behind a gingerbread facade at **Ivica i Marica** (Tkalčićeva 70, tel. 01/481-7321, www.ivicaimarica.com, 10 A.M.–11 P.M. Mon.–Fri., 9 A.M.–11 P.M. Sat., 11 A.M.–8 P.M. Sun., 20Kn) you might be expecting to find a cheesy tourist locale, but you'd be wrong. Locals love the place for their healthy no-preservative cakes and cookies and the nonsmoking atmosphere.

Fine Dining

Unless you eat dinner really early, you'll need to make reservations for **Takenoko** (Nova Ves 17, tel. 01/486-0530, www.takenoko.hr, 11 A.M.–1 A.M. Mon.–Sat., 11 A.M.–6 P.M. Sun., 85Kn), Zagreb's first sushi restaurant and in-crowd favorite. The sashimi and wok bowls are quite nice, but the American-style rolls are a bit overpriced for what you get. No reservation? Try snagging a seat at the bar.

If you can't figure out exactly what you're in the mood for, **Mano** (Medvedgradska 2, tel. 01/466-9432, www.mano.hr, noon–11 P.M. Mon.–Sat., 100Kn) can probably help you out with a menu featuring dishes influenced by Indian, Asian, Mediterranean, and local cuisines. Some of the dishes try just a bit too hard (and rarely impress) but the atmosphere—a candlelit brick-walled warehouse space—is one of the best in the city.

International

If your craving is for curry, pop by **Maharadža** (Opatovina 19, tel. 01/481-4305, noon–11 P.M. Tues.–Sun., 60Kn), an intimate and pretty good, if not very busy, Indian restaurant.

Once the sun goes down, **Plató** (Nova Ves 17, tel. 01/486-0721, 9 A.M.–1 A.M. Mon.–Sat., 60Kn) becomes a hip lounge space for throwing back cocktails. But if you're looking for breakfast, lunch, or dinner, the light-filled space (perfect for dining on a rainy day) has a good menu inspired by varied cuisines. From shrimp tempura to a club burger, it's all good, particularly the hot chocolate cake with vanilla-bean ice cream.

Local Cuisine

I've seen travelers walk away from the restaurant at **Ivica i Marica** (Tkalčićeva 70, tel. 01/481-7321, www.ivicaimarica.com, 10 A.M.–11 P.M. Mon.–Fri., 9 A.M.–11 P.M. Sat., 11 A.M.–8 P.M. Sun., 70Kn), located beside its excellent café, afraid the traditionally costumed waitstaff and homespun flavor of the wood-beamed restaurant spell tourist trap. But it's actually a favorite of locals too, with well-prepared regional dishes and quite a few vegetarian options.

Technically, it's a slight detour from Kaptol to **Kod Žaca** (Griskovićeva 4, tel. 01/468-4178, noon–midnight daily, 90Kn), or Žac's Place, but it's not far off the beaten tourist track. Look closely or you'll miss the small plaque that marks this little gem. Ask the owner, Žac, for his recommendation; if you're lucky you can try the duck raised by his mother. The atmosphere is traditional and the flavor is local, but the international clientele includes heavy hitting business executives and local celebrities.

Quick Bites

City Kebab (Tkalčićeva 27, 10 A.M.–11 P.M. daily, 20Kn) is the definition of "hole in the wall." This miniscule place is where to go for *doner* kebabs, mystery meat sandwiches that taste really good (the level of satisfaction tends to escalate with your level of drunkenness) and are slightly addictive.

Mangiare (Tkalčićeva 29, tel. 01/482-8173, 10 A.M.–11 P.M. Mon.–Sat., 1–11 P.M. Sun., 40Kn) is a cozy little pizzeria with a pleasant atmosphere and tasty brick oven–baked pizzas.

You'll find **Rubelj** (Dolac Market, 10 A.M.–midnight daily, 35Kn) restaurants all over Zagreb. Rubelj is almost synonymous with *čevapčići*, slightly spicy ground-meat rolls eaten with doughy bread. They also have a good selection of pizzas and other grilled meat dishes. The location next to Dolac has a large terrace for eating on the run in nicer weather.

For a really quick (and cheap) snack, pick up a *burek* from one of the bakeries lining **Dolac Market** or a piece of fresh fruit and a small bag of nuts from one of the vendors.

A much-needed addition to Zagreb's fast-food scene, **Daily Fresh** (Frane Petrića 1, at the corner with Ilica, tel. 01/639-7111, 8 A.M.–11 P.M. daily, 35Kn) makes sandwiches and salads as well as to-go coffee (a relatively new concept in town). The chain has several locations across town but the most convenient for tourists is located steps from Trg bana Jelačića on Ilica.

GORNJI GRAD
Fine Dining

Built into the old city walls just steps from the Kamenita vrata, **Noće** (Kamenita 5, tel. 01/485-1394, www.noce.hr, noon–midnight Mon.–Thurs., noon–1 A.M. Fri.–Sat., 85Kn) serves up Italian-inspired dishes like homemade green ravioli with lobster crème, a good grilled chicken salad, and lots of yummy crostini and bruschetta options for a young, hip crowd.

Though actually a short drive out of the upper town, **Bistro Apetit** (Jurjevska 65a, 01/467-7335, 9 A.M.–midnight Tues.–Sun., 90Kn) is a chic slow-food restaurant in a modern light-filled space. Don't let the description scare you off, though. The place is elegant but

a place to wet your whistle in Gornji Grad

unpretentious, and the out-of-this-world food is worth the not-outrageous prices.

Local Cuisine

Pod gričkim topom (Zakmardijeve stube 5, tel. 01/483-3607, 11 A.M.–midnight Mon.–Sat., 150Kn) serves up slightly overpriced Croatian comfort food just steps from Kula Lotrščak, or Burglars' Tower. The terrace is the best spot to dine in nice weather, with a great view of the lower town. The restaurant has been heavily covered in guides and articles, though, so if you're looking for an insider find, this is not it.

It seems apropos that **Stara Vura** (Opatička 20, tel. 01/485-1368, www.stara-vura.hr, noon–midnight Mon.–Sat., 110Kn) shares an entrance with the Zagreb City Museum. The ancient brick domed interior is like a medieval cellar. The dishes are good, though a bit expensive. You'll get the most for your money if you dine here on Friday or Saturday night when a band of Gypsy *tambura* musicians descend on the place, singing lively folk music.

Didov san (Mletačka ulica 11, tel. 01/485-1154, www.konoba-didovsan.com, 10 A.M.–11 P.M. Mon.–Sat., 10 A.M.–10 P.M. Sun., 95Kn) is filled with regional touches, from the dark-wood and embroidered-tablecloth interior to the food. Specializing in Dalmatian cuisine, there's a good selection of fish dishes and even a couple of escargot options for gourmands. The *janjetina ispod peke* (oven-baked lamb) is worth ordering ahead.

Quick Bites

Claiming to be the oldest café in Zagreb, **Pod Starim Krovovima** (Basaričekova 9, tel. 01/485-1342, 8 A.M.–11 P.M. Mon.–Sat., 18Kn) has been serving guests since 1830. Today the space is bright and friendly with a new exhibition of art on its walls every month. Have a beer and snack on *hrenovke* (hot dogs), *kranske* (a type of regional sausage), or a sandwich.

DONJI GRAD
Cafés and Desserts

If you're window shopping on Ilica, stop at **Vincek** (Ilica 18, tel. 01/483-3612, www.vincek.com.hr, 8:30 A.M.–11 P.M. Mon.–Sat., 20Kn), a long-running Zagreb institution, for cakes, cookies, and ice cream.

Crepes filled with banana and vanilla sauce might just be the closest thing to dessert perfection at (**Crepes de Paris** (Oktogon br. 5, tel. 091/400-1033, 7 A.M.–11 P.M. Sun.–Thurs., 7 A.M.–midnight Fri.–Sat., 18Kn) on Cvjetni trg (Flower Square). The little stand offers a lot of other options for filling *palačinke*, the local name for crepes, like chocolate sauce, nutella, nuts, and fruity jams.

Pass on the cakes at (**Millennium** (Bogovićeva 7, tel. 01/481-0850, 8 A.M.–11 P.M. daily, 8Kn). They're good, but they can't come close to the creamy gelato-style ice cream in dozens of flavors.

Fine Dining

While it might be a slight stretch to say the cuisine of (**Škola** (Bogovićeva 7/2, tel. 01/482-8196, www.skolaloungebar.com, 10 A.M.–1 A.M. Mon.–Sat., 11 A.M.–midnight

ZAGREB'S SOLAR SYSTEM

Prizemljeno Sunce, the center of Zagreb's solar system

When you're having a drink or snack on Bogovićeva, make sure to look out for the large golden ball, actually a sculpture by Ivan Kožarić, titled *Prizemljeno Sunce* (Grounded Sun). First exhibited in 1971, the ball, almost seven feet in diameter, changed location several times before it landed in one of Zagreb's busiest pedestrian streets in 1994. In the early years of the new millennium, Dawor Preis began placing models of the planets of the solar system around town with little or no publicity. Even most locals aren't aware of his installation, entitled *Nine Views*. The size and distance of all the models are in scale with the "sun," the *Prizemljeno Sunce*. If you'd like to discover all nine models, someone has tracked them down at www.phy.hr/~mpozek/planeti.

Sun., 70Kn) classifies as gourmet, the restaurant gets bumped into this category if only on the basis of bang for the buck. With excellent food, attentive waitstaff, and an ultra-modern gallery-style space, this lounge bar/disco by night, restaurant by day and evening is one of the city's most overlooked eateries. A small black sign near the Millennium ice cream parlor will lead you behind the Profil Megastore in a building that used to be a school, hence the name.

International

Located in a dark but swank space at the bottom of Branimir Centar, **Opium** (Branimirova 29, tel. 01/461-5679, www.opium.hr, 11 A.M.–midnight Mon.–Sat., 11 A.M.–11:30 P.M. Sun., 70Kn) offers food that won't blow you away, but if you're in the mood for Thai it's your only option.

If you ask locals for their favorite Chinese restaurant, they'll almost always say **Asia** (Šenoina 1, tel. 01/484-1218, noon–midnight daily, 70Kn). It so happens several Chinese nationals in Zagreb say the same. If you're a big fan of Mandarin cuisine, feel free to order dishes not listed on the menu.

Local Cuisine

The interior of **Purger** (Petrinjska 33, tel. 01/481-0713, 7 A.M.–11 P.M. Mon.–Sat., 50Kn) is pretty basic, but the hearty local dishes are well prepared and well priced. There's also a terrace.

At **Pivnica Palmeta** (Palmotićeva 5, tel. 091/579-4120, 10 A.M.–10 P.M. Mon.–Sat., 55Kn), a block's walk from Trg bana Jelačića, near the Jurišićeva post office, the food is hearty and good and the service is informal and cheeky. Sophisticated it is not, but it's hard to knock its value for money and the '70s communist vibe, disappearing fast in a city bent on keeping up with the rest of Europe. You'll leave with your stomach full and your wallet not much lighter.

For a more upmarket local experience, **Stari Fijaker** (Mesnička 6, tel. 01/483-3829, www.starifijaker.hr, 7 A.M.–11 P.M. daily, 85Kn) has Croatian staples like *punjeni paprika* (stuffed peppers) and *sarma* (pork and rice wrapped in cabbage leaves).

Quick Bites

Donji Grad is filled with good options for fast food. If late nights and panini-style sandwiches are your thing, **Pinguin** (Nikole Tesle 7, tel. 01/481-1446, 8:30 A.M.–5 A.M. Mon.–Sat., 7 P.M.–3 A.M. Sun., 18Kn) will satisfy, with huge hot circles of bread filled with basic toppings like ham, cheese, and fresh tomatoes.

Ham Ham (Varšavska 8, tel. 01/483-0483, 9 A.M.–11 P.M. Mon.–Sat., 35Kn) was serving burgers to locals long before McDonald's came to town. The restaurant, a bit hidden at the back of a passage, was recently renovated and looks more like a chic lounge than a fast-food place. Burgers with Ham Ham's special sauce are served on china plates and you get a real glass with your drink. Ham Ham is also the best place to get a good, reasonable breakfast or brunch, with eggs any style, bacon, and a side of fresh tomatoes.

Flores (Frane Petriča 1, tel. 01/481-9272, 7 A.M.–11 P.M. Mon.–Sat., 9 A.M.–11 P.M. Sun.,

30Kn) is a chic café that also sells a few good sandwiches for a meal on the go.

Less than a block from Trg bana Jelačića is **Mimiće** (Jurišićeva 21, 8 A.M.–9 P.M. Mon.–Fri., 8 A.M.–5 P.M. Sat., 20Kn), a fish restaurant that is low on atmosphere but high in character. If you don't mind standing up, this Croatian version of fish-and-chips is a great value.

For those who'd like a chair with their fish, **Gostionica Tip-Top** (Gundulićeva 18, tel. 01/483-0349, 7 A.M.–10 P.M. daily, 40Kn), locally known as Blato (mud), serves excellent and very well-priced fish dishes. The unpretentious *kavana* was very popular with Croatian artists and has immortalized the poet Tin Ujević on the front window. The cuisine comes from the island of Korčula, with dishes like *pašticada* and *bakalar* (cod) every Friday. There's also a good selection of Dalmatian wines.

A bit on the pricey side for quick bites, but worth a mention for the sunny French bistro-style atmosphere and super brunch-type dishes, **Le Bistro** (Mihanovićeva 1, tel. 01/456-6666, 9 A.M.–11 P.M. daily, 85Kn) in the Regent Esplanade hotel is a great way to while away a Sunday morning.

Vegan

A macrobiotic restaurant in a small but sleek space, **Nova restoran** (Ilica 72, tel. 01/481-0059, www.biovega.hr, 9 A.M.–10 P.M. Mon.–Sat., 55Kn) offers an impressive range of vegan dishes with dozens of delicious spins on tofu, seitan, and vegetables.

OUTSIDE THE CENTER
Fine Dining

Marcellino (Jurjevska 71, tel. 01/467-7111, noon–11 P.M. Mon.–Sat., 120Kn) has long been Zagreb's only truly fine-dining restaurant (read: small portions and creative cuisine), though Bistro Apetit is giving it a run for its money. The space is large and modern and prettiest at night when the trees outside the large windows are lit from below. The food is very good, with what seems like four chefs participating in every dish (you can see them working from the dining room), but the prices are high.

Dubravkin Put (Dubravkin put 2, tel. 01/483-4975, 10 A.M.–midnight daily, 115Kn) is the city's nicest fish restaurant with food to match. The decor is simple but the vibe is luxe to the extreme.

International
Mex Cantina (Savska cesta 154, tel. 01/619-2156, www.asker.com/mex-cantina, 9 A.M.–11 P.M. daily, 70Kn) has the most authentic Mexican food in Zagreb and if you want a fajita, it's probably worth the hike out to Savska. If you're planning on partying at Movie Pub, it's practically across the street.

A tiny Italian restaurant, **Fellini** (Savska 90, tel. 01/617-7545, www.fellini.hr, 11 A.M.–11 P.M. Mon.–Fri., noon–11 P.M. Sat.–Sun., 60Kn) is usually full with patrons who know the food and service are consistent and the wine list isn't too shabby either.

Local Cuisine
If you can't make it to Dalmatia, a meal at (**Dida** (Petrova 176, tel. 01/233-5693, 9 A.M.–11 P.M. Mon.–Sat., 9 A.M.–10 P.M. Sun., 100Kn) is the next best thing. With a rustic coastal interior and fish you select from a bed of ice before it's cooked, Dida serves meals that are pricey but always excellent quality.

Quick Bites
Near Cibona Tower, (**Karijola** (Kranjčevićeva 16a, tel. 01/366-7044, 9 A.M.–midnight daily, 45Kn) serves pizza, but not the kind you ordered at 2 A.M. for sustenance during a study session. Their clay oven–baked pizzas have a thin crispy crust and super-fresh ingredients. The pizza with mozzarella, tomato, and fresh basil hits the spot on a hot summer day.

Only a couple of blocks from the Sheraton, **Canzona** (Ivana Šveara 9, tel. 01/461-7777, 9 A.M.–11 P.M. Mon.–Sat., noon–11 P.M. Sun., 55Kn) is as cute as restaurants get. The walls are painted to depict quaint buildings, and in the lantern light it really does feel like you're eating in an Italian courtyard. The pasta and pizza dishes are very good and their tiramisu is a sweet ending to your meal.

Information and Services

TOURIST AND TRAVEL INFORMATION
The main **tourist office** (Trg bana Jelačića 11, tel. 01/481-4051, info@zagreb-touristinfo.hr, www.zagreb-touristinfo.hr, 8:30 A.M.–8 P.M. Mon.–Fri., 9 A.M.–5 P.M. Sat., 10 A.M.–2 P.M. Sun.) is located on Trg bana Jelačića and provides some nice color brochures, featuring maps and walks around town, free of charge. The office also provides information on events and happenings around town and sells the Zagreb Card (90Kn), which includes free city transport, a 50 percent discount on museums and tours, and discounts at other locations throughout the city during a 72-hour period.

GUIDED TOURS
If you'd like someone to take you around town, the tourist office can hook you up with a private guide or you can hop on the **Zagreb City Tour** (tel. 01/369-4333, www.ibus.hr, 10 A.M. daily Apr. 1–Oct. 31, other times by arrangement, 165Kn per person, discount with the Zagreb Card), run by iBus; the tour departs from Bakačeva Street near the cathedral.

A slightly quirkier option is the **Segway City Tour** (tel. 01/301-0390, www.segwaycitytourzagreb.com, from 300Kn depending on tour and number of people), which offers several pre-planned tours or custom tours depending on your interests. The tours start and end at the Regent Esplanade hotel and more information is available from the concierges at the Regent Esplanade and the Best Western Hotel Astoria as well as the tourist office on Trg bana Jelačića.

BANKS AND CURRENCY EXCHANGE

It's best to avoid changing money at hotels due to the usually poor exchange rate; most banks will exchange money, as will exchange offices (look for the *mjenjačnica* signs), who take about a 1.5 percent commission. Major banks are Zagrebačka Banka, Privedna Banka (PBZ), and Raiffeisen. If you need to exchange money outside of business hours, head to the bus station or the post office next to the train station for 24-hour service. Also, ATMs (labeled *bankomat*) around town accept most major cards. There's one conveniently located on Trg bana Jelačića, as well as many other locations around the center. Don't expect to find one in Gornji Grad, however.

INTERNET ACCESS AND COMMUNICATIONS

The main post office (Branimirova 4, 24 hours) is located next to the train station. Here, as well as at the post office at Jurišićeva 13 (7 A.M.–9 P.M. Mon.–Fri., 7 A.M.–7 P.M. Sat., 8 A.M.–2 P.M. Sun.) have metered booths for international telephone calls. Other post offices are located around town—just look for the yellow Pošta signs.

While more and more hotels and hostels are offering free Internet connections, there are several places to go if you're in a pinch.

For the whole package (computer and access) with an alternative, gay-friendly vibe, try **M.a.m.a.** (Preradovićeva 18, tel. 01/485-6400, www.mi2.hr, 10 A.M.–10 P.M. Mon.–Sat., 4–10 P.M. Sun., 10Kn per hour), which also has fax and copying services on the premises. **Sublink Internet Centar** (Teslina 12, tel. 01/481-1329, www.sublink.hr, 9 A.M.–10 P.M. Mon.–Sat., 3–10 P.M. Sun., 15Kn per hour, student discount) is another option nearby, with an in-house café if you need a shot of caffeine. If you have your laptop or wireless handheld with you, order up a drink at **Škola Lounge Bar** (Bogovićeva 7, tel. 01/482-8196) and surf using the bar's Wi-Fi Internet access. Wi-Fi is beginning to pop up at more and more locations around town.

LAUNDRY SERVICES

Washing, dry-cleaning, ironing, and basic mending services can be found at **Doratex** (Draškovićeva 31, tel. 01/461-2990, 7 A.M.–7 P.M. Mon.–Fri., 8 A.M.–noon Sat., 6–18Kn per item) or **Petecin Zdenka** (Kaptol 11, tel. 01/481-4802, 8 A.M.–8 P.M. Mon.–Fri., 8 A.M.–3 P.M. Sat., 6–20Kn per item).

LEFT LUGGAGE

The main bus station (Avenija M. Držića bb, tel. 060/313-333, www.akz.hr, 6 A.M.–10 P.M. daily, 1.20Kn for up to 15 kg per hour) and train station (Trg Kralja Tomislava 12, tel. 060/333-444, 24 hours) have left luggage offices with cheap rates for stowing your bags.

EMERGENCY SERVICES

Croatia's emergency number is 112, though you can also dial each service directly: ambulance (94), fire (93), and police (92). The main police station (tel. 01/456-3311) is at Petrinjska 30. If you find yourself in need of a doctor in the middle of the night, the clinic of the Sveti Duh hospital (Sveti Duh 64, tel. 01/371-2111) is open 24 hours. There are several all-night pharmacies in Zagreb, though the most central is at Ilica 43 (tel. 01/484-8450).

Getting There and Around

GETTING THERE
Air
Located 17 kilometers from the center, Zagreb's small Pleso Airport (tel. 060/320-320, www.zagreb-airport.hr) is easy to find your way around, and out of. Croatia Airlines (tel. 01/487-2727 or 01/616-0215, www.croatiaairlines.hr) is the major carrier to and from the airport.

From the airport, a taxi to the center should cost around 200–250Kn. If you take a taxi, make sure the driver starts the meter and ask for a receipt. A cheaper option is to take the Croatia Airlines bus, which leaves the airport every half hour or hour (check the schedule at www.plesoprijevoz.hr/schedulezg.htm). The price is only 30Kn, payable to the driver, and takes about 30 minutes to the main bus station.

Train
Zagreb's main train station (Trg Kralja Tomislava 12, tel. 060/333-444) is conveniently located in the center of the city; unlike in many European cities, it is located in a safe area. Trains, run by Hrvatske željeznice (Croatian Railways, tel. 060/333-444, www.hznet.hr), are usually on time and are a great way of getting around the Zagreb area. You can also pick up multiple daily connections to regions around Croatia and Slovenia. Inter-Rail passes are valid in Croatia, though Eurail is not.

Tickets should be purchased at the ticket counter to save a little money; tickets bought from the conductor will be slightly higher. You should also be aware that there are slow trains *(putnički)* that stop at every station along the way, and inter-city trains (IC), which are more expensive but usually worth the money in time savings.

You can purchase a timetable at the station, though your best bet is to check out Croatian Railways' website. Make sure to give yourself a few extra minutes to board since the Zagreb train station can be more than a little confusing at times.

Bus
The city has a large and busy bus station (Avenija M. Držića bb, tel. 060/313-333, www.akz.hr) with lots of connections. Though the inter-city buses are run by multiple companies, the system actually runs pretty smoothly, as long as you don't get ruffled by the occasional unscheduled stop to drop regular customers off closer to their houses.

Car
Highways into Zagreb from Slovenia are quite good, with most of the Ljubljana to Zagreb highway (A3, approximately 1.5–2 hours between the two capitals) having been recently completed. From the Ljubljana border, drive straight until you see white signs marked with the word Centar, directing you toward the center of town. If you're traveling from Zagreb to Maribor, take the A2, also about a two-hour journey between the two cities.

GETTING AROUND
Tram and Bus
Since Zagreb's trams only operate in the central zone of the city, you need not worry about getting too lost. The main hubs for trams are at the train station and Trg bana Jelačića, with large maps displayed at these major stops to help you find your way. Buses will take you into the suburbs of Zagreb.

Regular service for both buses and trams is from early morning to 11:20 P.M., when night services take effect. During the day, tram service is very frequent (around every 10–15 minutes), though night trams and buses are terribly confusing to figure out, with crazy schedules and different routes than those on the regular service route. If you find yourself needing a bus or tram late at night, the best thing to do is ask. As Croatians are usually friendly people and a large percentage of the population under 40 speaks English, you shouldn't have a problem.

To travel on buses and trams, buy tickets at newspaper stands or directly from the driver. You can buy tickets per journey (6Kn from the kiosk, 10Kn from the driver, valid one-way for 90 minutes) or per day (*dnevne karte*, 25Kn), or buy a **Zagreb Card** from the tourist office—this includes city transport for 72 hours as well as discounts to museums. Once you board the tram or bus, simply validate your ticket by punching it in the machine onboard.

Taxi

There are numerous taxi stands in Zagreb. The two most central and convenient taxi stands are on Trg bana Jelačića next to the Varteks department store and on Gajeva next to the pedestrian zone. You'll also find them in front of the main train and bus stations as well as in front of hotels. Alternatively, call 970 or 01/660-0671 to reserve a taxi. (You will not find taxis driving around waiting to be flagged down—the person wildly gesturing at cabs from the sidewalk is easily pegged as a tourist.)

Taxis in Zagreb are incredibly expensive, and unfortunately some drivers like to get the best of foreigners. The standard rate is 25Kn to start and 7Kn for every kilometer thereafter (rates are increased at night and on Sundays and holidays). If you try using a few words of Croatian you'll lessen your chances of being taken for a more expensive ride than you planned. Also make sure the driver turns on the meter and ask for a receipt.

Most drivers, however, are friendly and honest. While tipping is not standard, it is customary to round up when paying your fare.

Car

While driving on Croatia's highways is quite easy and comfortable, driving in-town is often a stressful, wild tangle of cars. Traffic in Zagreb is nearly always bad from 8 A.M. to around 6 or 7 P.M., unless of course you visit in July and August when it seems like the entire city is at the coast. The major tips for in-town driving: Pay attention and remember that the majority of drivers do not obey the rules.

If you need to rent a car in Zagreb, Budget Rent-a-Car (www.budget.hr) and Avis (www.avis.com.hr) have locations in Pleso Airport and the Sheraton. The wonderful service Rent-a-Smart (Ivana Kukuljevića 32, tel. 01/487-6172, www.rentasmart.com.hr, 10 A.M.–8 P.M. Mon.–Sat.) rents Smart cars from one day to one year, making getting around town a cinch.

Parking in Zagreb is scarce and not for those averse to parallel parking, so you'll want to find somewhere to leave the car and traverse the city center by foot or with the help of trams (if you chose the Smart car, however, you'll find a few more spots to leave the car). If you do need to park in Zagreb, remember that each zone is subject to different rules, with first-zone areas allowing a maximum of only one hour. Find a parking meter, placed at intervals along the street, and pay, then place the receipt on your dashboard from inside the car. Or pay your parking via cell phone—send your license plate number via a text message to 101 (Zone 1, one-hour maximum), 102 (Zone 2, two-hour maximum), or 103 (Zone 3, three-hour maximum). It is charged to your cell phone immediately; it's either added to your bill or, if you have a prepaid card, deducted from the balance. Lately the city has been quite tow-happy, so make sure the place you park is legal.

Around Zagreb

SAMOBOR

Since the early 19th century, Samobor has lured travelers to its charming streets and the tranquil mountains that surround it. Though today it is mainly a destination for Zagreb residents looking to get away from it all, in the past its importance and culture rivaled that of its much larger neighbor.

There are a few things in this gingerbread town that are considered typical Samobor. The most famous is the *kremšnita*, a flaky square of crust topped with vanilla custard, though its name suggests the origin may be Austrian (but don't mention that to the locals). They also make a big deal over their crystal, though you'd probably be better off toting home some local *bermet*, touted as an aperitif—or a digestif, which might be a better term given how strong it is, or *samoborska muštarda*, a very sharp mustard with a hint of grape.

One of the best times to come is during **Samoborski fašnik,** or carnival, when the town hosts hundreds of revelers with all kinds of performances and lots of activities for kids. Samobor's version of carnival is decidedly more family-friendly than its better-known cousins.

If you miss *fašnik* there are several other festivals worth checking out. The Samoborski proljetni sajam (Samobor spring fair) features stands with local food products and handiwork, while the square is popping with fireworks on Dan Grada (Day of the Town, July 26), and Samoborska glazbena jesen, Samobor's autumn music festival, brings some excellent musicians to town. Check with the **tourist office** (Trg Kralja Tomislava 5, tel. 01/336-0044, www.tz-samobor.hr, 8 A.M.–7 P.M. Mon.–Fri., 9 A.M.–7 P.M. Sat., 10 A.M.–7 P.M. Sun.) for more information.

Sights

After admiring the pretty buildings and the mountains from **Trg Kralja Tomislava,** the main square and center of the tiny town, head to the **Gradski muzej** (Town Museum, Livadićeva 7, tel. 01/336-1014, 9 A.M.–3 P.M. Tues.–Fri., 9 A.M.–1 P.M. Sat.–Sun., 12Kn) next to the Hotel Lavica. The museum was home to composer Ferdo Livadić, who once hosted his friend Franz Liszt here. There's not too much to see here, besides some furniture and decorations from local families and a decent exhibit of agricultural tools.

Heading back across the square towards the parish church you'll pass the **Muzej Marton** (Marton Museum, Jurjevska 7, tel. 01/332-6426, www.muzej-marton.hr, 10 A.M.–1 P.M. Sat.–Sun., 15Kn), which will delight fans of glass and porcelain with a large display including pieces by Meissen, Sèvres, and plates that once belonged to Tsar Nicholas I.

The **Fotogalerija Lang** (Langova 15, tel. 01/336-2884, 11 A.M.–1 P.M. and 4–7 P.M. Sat.–Sun. and by appt.), tucked in an alleyway, hosts surprisingly good contemporary

Samobor's Gradski muzej

view of mountains from Samobor's town center

If you really want to explore the excellent **hiking** options around town, pick up a *planinarska karta* (mountain map) from the tourist office on Trg Kralja Tomislava.

Samobor is the entrance to the Žumberak region of inland Croatia, with a wonderful nature park (www.ppzsg.org) and some great ecotourism sites.

Accommodations

If you have a car, staying in Samobor, where you'll get more for your money, can be a much better option than Zagreb.

The **Hotel Livadić** (Trg Kralja Tomislava 1, tel. 01/336-5850, www.hotel-livadic.hr, 455Kn d., including breakfast) is the nicest accommodation in Samobor, with quaint rooms right on Trg Kralja Tomislava, the main square.

The **Hotel Lavica** (Ferde Livadića 5, tel. 01/336-8000, www.lavica-hotel.hr, 291Kn d., including breakfast) is somewhat more basic but the price is better and the location is only a few steps away from Trg Kralja Tomislava.

Food

For local flavor at lunch or dinner, the **Samoborska Pivnica** (Šmihenova 3, tel. 01/336-1623, www.samoborska-pivnica.hr, 9 A.M.–11 P.M. Mon.–Fri., 9 A.M.–midnight Sat.–Sun., 70Kn) serves up stomach-filling dishes in a cavelike space. The **Hotel Lavica** (Ferde Livadića 5, tel. 01/336-8000, www.lavica-hotel.hr, 75Kn) restaurant is even nicer, with a dark-wood interior and a quiet location next to the Town Museum.

Zeleni Papar (Ante Starčevića 17, tel. 01/336-3893, www.zelenipapar.hr, 11 A.M.–11 P.M. Mon.–Sat., closed Aug., 80Kn) doesn't look all that special, but it has some of the best food in Samobor, with homemade *kulen* (salami), wine goulash, and super *biftek* (steak).

For a quicker bite, try the **Pizzeria Napoli** (Grada Wirgesa 6, tel. 01/336-0072, noon–10 P.M. Mon.–Sat., 40Kn) for pizzas and pasta dishes.

Information and Services

Located conveniently on Trg Kralja Tomislava,

photography exhibits. A short walk away, on the northeastern side of the square, is the **Galerija Prica** (Trg Matice hrvatske 3, tel. 01/333-6214, 9 A.M.–3 P.M. Tues.–Thurs., 1–7 P.M. Fri., 10 A.M.–1 P.M. Sat.–Sun., 15Kn), which displays paintings by primary-color fan and local artist Zlatko Prica, and haunting photography from his equally talented daughter Vesna.

The town has two nice Baroque churches worth a peek if you have the extra time: the 17th-century **Crkva Sv. Anastazije** and the 18th-century church of the **Franjevački Samostan** (Franciscan Monastery). But if you're tight on time, make a beeline for the **Anindol** forest on Tepec Hill. It's full of paths to explore, but the best two are the winding **Križni put**, which puts you at the tiny **Kapelica sv. Jurja** (Chapel of St. George) in less than half an hour, or the path to Samobor's **Stari Grad**. Stari Grad is really just the ruins of the town's 13th-century castle, but the view is worth the hike and the ruins are quite peaceful.

Trg Kralja Tomislava, the main square in Samobor

the **tourist office** (Trg Kralja Tomislava 5, tel. 01/336-0044, www.tz-samobor.hr, 8 A.M.–7 P.M. Mon.–Fri., 9 A.M.–7 P.M. Sat., 10 A.M.–7 P.M. Sun.) sells maps, including special versions for hiking. They also hand out free brochures and information and can help you arrange accommodation.

Getting There and Around

Samobor is a little over 20 kilometers west of Zagreb. If you're driving, take the A3 toward Ljubljana. The trip should take about 30 minutes, but heavy traffic on the road sometimes makes it a bit longer. Buses run by the Samoborček company (tel. 01/333-5170, www.samoborcek.hr) leave Zagreb's main bus station and the Črnomerec tram terminal. There are dozens of connections daily, taking about 45 minutes, and costing around 35Kn each way depending on where you get on. When you get to Samobor, from the bus station it is only a five-minute walk to the main square, Trg Kralja Tomislava.

PLEŠIVIČKA WINE ROUTE

The best wine route in the area is the Plešivička Wine Route. You can pick it up at Rude, a few kilometers southwest of Samobor. The roads are well marked; you can get additional information and a list of wineries online at www.zagrebacka-zupanija.hr/vina/eng. However, it's best not to plan too much and just enjoy the drive of around 20 or so kilometers through vineyards and villages. The wineries are marked with little signs declaring *vino*. Though none of them hold regular opening hours, despite some claiming they do, it's a nice drive hunting down a spot to buy some wine.

Most of the growers will offer you a tasting before you buy, which is important given that the quality of the wine will vary greatly. However, it's pretty cheap and if you happen to be traveling the road in autumn, you'll run into Portugizac Plešivička, the local version of Beaujolais Nouveau.

There are two nice places to stop for lunch along the way: **Restoran Ivančić** (Plešivica 45, tel. 01/629-3303, call for hours) with its vineyard-view terrace or **Boltina Hiža** (Pl. Prekrižje 12, tel. 01/629-3115, call for hours, closed Mon,).

ZAPREŠIĆ

The main attraction in the small town of Zaprešić, 18 kilometers northwest of Zagreb, is the **Jelačić Novi dvori,** a well-preserved feudal estate that covers 50 acres. There's also a small museum, the **Matija Skurjeni Museum** (Aleja Ðure Jelačića 8, tel. 01/331-0540, www.muzej-matija-skurjeni.hr, 10Kn), with a cheerful display of naive art, an impressive manor house, a chapel and the grand **Jelačić family tomb.** Hours are 9 A.M.–3 P.M. Tuesday and Thursday, noon–6 P.M. Wednesday and Friday in summer and 11 A.M.–5 P.M. Wednesday and Friday in winter, 9 A.M.–2 P.M. Saturday, and 9 A.M.–noon Sunday.

Nearby is a well-maintained **golf complex,** though it's really little more than a driving range. A short drive south, the **Zajarki Lake** has a nice fish farm and fishing society.

If you'd like to stay in Zaprešić or just want a bite while you're there, the **Trajbar Team** (Ulica bana J. Jelačića 199, tel. 01/331-0838, info@kk-trajbar-team.hr, www.kk-trajbar-team.hr, 312Kn d.) horse farm offers nice meals and rooms in a rural setting. If you'd like to try out your equestrian skills, the farm also offers lessons for beginners and trail rides for the more experienced.

Zaprešić is accessible by bus and train, with frequent connections since many people work in Zagreb. It's a 30-minute drive from Zagreb (take Ilica out of town and follow the signs for Zaprešić).

MARIJA BISTRICA

Thirty-two kilometers north of Zagreb is Marija Bistrica, whose hilltop **Hodočasnička crkva Marije Bistričke** (Pilgrimage Church of St. Mary of Bistrica, tel. 049/468-380, www.info-marija-bistrica.hr, contact tourist board for hours and pilgrimages) has turned into a destination for the devout, particularly between Whitsunday (Pentecost) and the end of October. The church itself is attractive, designed in the late 18th century by Bollé, who built Zagreb's cathedral. But the pilgrims come not so much for the church as for the **Black Madonna,** a 15th-century dark wooden statue of the Virgin. Legend has it that the statue was bricked into the church wall in the 17th century to protect it from the Turks. Some three decades later, a beam of light revealed its hiding place. Locals declared it a miracle and the bishop of Zagreb spread the news, hoping to promote the town as a spiritual center for pilgrims.

His efforts paid off and today the Black Madonna, who also survived an 1880 fire that only added to her aura, brings busloads of tourists to the otherwise tiny town.

Behind the huge **amphitheater,** built for a visit by the pope in 1998, a path leads up **Kalvarija** (Calvary Hill), passing the Stations of the Cross to a very nice view of the town at the top.

If you have time and your own car, take a leisurely drive north to **Belec** to visit the gorgeous 1675 Baroque church of **Marija Snježna** (Our Lady of the Snow). The outside is plain and unassuming but the inside is filled with paintings, gilt, and heavily carved statues and altars. Though the church is only officially open on Sundays, knock at the white house just below the front gate of the church and ask for Ivo, the bellringer. It's his job to unlock the church for visitors, so don't be embarrassed.

The rooms at **Lojzekova hiža** (Gusakovec 116, Gornja Stubica, tel. 049/469-325, info@lojzekovahiza.com, www.lojzekovahiza.com, 199Kn d., including breakfast), west of Marija Bistrica, are pretty basic, but the typical Zagorje farmhouse, the warm and friendly owners, and their soul-warming comfort food make an overnight in the area a pleasing idea.

If you'd like to visit Marija Bistrica, there are multiple connections by bus daily to and from Zagreb (40 minutes). To visit the church at Belec, about 15 kilometers north of Marija Bistrica, follow the road to Zlatar and then follow signs for Belec.

LJUBLJANA

With a cultural menu to rival much larger capitals, a funky nightlife, and a strong sense of self (despite being squeezed in the middle of various ruling empires throughout history), Ljubljana is a European capital minute in size but big on character. The city is charming precisely because it is small. You can get intimate with Ljubljana, see the sights, and still have time left to discover a few gems of your own.

Most impressive about Ljubljana may be the tremendous mark made on its streetscapes and buildings by the country's most famous architect, Jože Plečnik. Whether you admire his style, heavily influenced by the classicists, or not, it's impossible not to admire the sheer amount of work he undertook during his lifetime and his vision for a grand city, even if it is quite small. Ljubljana is also full of good restaurants, lots of clubs and bars for evenings out, and plenty of stops to interest younger visitors. Though it's several hundred thousand residents smaller than Zagreb to the south (Ljubljana has close to 270,000 in the metro area), it's more developed, hitting just the right chord between East and West.

Ljubljana hasn't been overrun by tourists... yet. It's still overlooked by lots of visitors, like Germans and Austrians traveling down to Dalmatia who just drive straight through. You can easily see the city in one day and still have time to explore it further or get out into the countryside for a day trip. Travelers that take the time to wander the Old Town, eat in the restaurants, and browse the antiques markets and tiny galleries will find a warm, friendly

© J. SKOK/SLOVENIAN TOURIST BOARD

HIGHLIGHTS

◐ **Tromostovje:** Also known as the Triple Bridge, this is a trademark of the city, built by architect Jože Plečnik (page 48).

◐ **Zmajski Most:** Stopping for a photo op on this bridge, famous for its iconic dragons, is a must (page 50).

◐ **Stolnica sveti Nikolaja:** The city's cathedral has all the things you've come to expect in European churches: frescoes, gilt, and sculptures. It also has some unexpected features, like fabulous bronze doors (page 51).

◐ **Ljubljanski Grad:** The views from this hilltop castle complex make it worth the hike (page 51).

◐ **Gornji trg:** The one-stop shop of the Old Town, this picturesque square and its extension, Levstikov trg, are home to some of the city's most beautiful facades and churches (page 52).

◐ **Krakovo:** A laid-back fishermen's settlement turned into a quarter for artists on a pension, Krakovo is filled with peasant-style homes, a few Roman ruins, and lots of character (page 54).

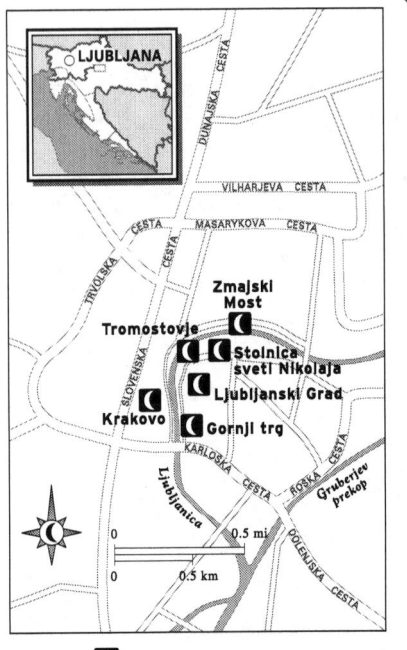

LOOK FOR ◐ TO FIND RECOMMENDED SIGHTS, ACTIVITIES, DINING, AND LODGING.

town, slightly quirky, always confident in the treasure that is Ljubljana.

HISTORY

The Romans came to the area in the 1st century A.D. and called the city Emona; an invasion by Attila the Hun in the 5th century destroyed most of the Roman structures. The city lay fairly barren until the 12th century, when a new settlement was built below the castle by Carniolan aristocracy. In the 14th century the Hapsburgs took over and didn't let go, except during a brief reign by Napoleon when Ljubljana was capital of the Illyrian provinces between 1809 and 1813.

The age of rail travel transformed Ljubljana, making it a major center of culture and tourism. An earthquake in 1895 damaged the city's buildings, many beyond repair, but made room for an even grander city, marked by over-the-top Secessionist buildings.

Ljubljana, once a stop on the Orient Express, flourished until World War II. Even after inclusion in Tito's Yugoslavia, the city grew substantially as people from rural villages moved into town for factory jobs, changing the landscape of modern Ljubljana, whose suburbs are marked by huge apartment buildings.

It's always been a prosperous city, relishing in its location between East and West, accepted by both sides as one of their own and capitalizing on that singularity. As the capital of the first former Yugoslav republic to enter the European Union (in 2004), Ljubljana is poised to use its position to even more advantage.

PLANNING YOUR TIME

If you have two or three days to spend in Ljubljana, you won't regret it. That said, the city is very small and easily doable on foot, and it's possible to pack in the highlights in one full day.

A quick tour should hit Prešernov Trg, Ljubljanski Grad, and the Old Town (Mestni trg, Stari trg, and Gornji trg), with a stop at the Zmajski Most for a photograph. Top off the day with a good dinner and at least one coffee and cake. If you have another day, fit in some of Ljubljana's excellent museums, galleries, and a bit of shopping. With a third day, spend some time in Tivoli Gardens and hopefully a visit to the charming quarter of Krakovo.

The city is beautiful all throughout the year, though summer is probably the most fun, with warm evenings and long days perfect for strolling along the river and sipping a wine at an outdoor café. December is also nice, with the festive decorations and holiday market making the already gingerbread-vibe city an excellent holiday getaway.

ORIENTATION

The Ljubljanica River divides the city into two distinct sides. To the east, you'll find Ljubljana's most ancient core, with the castle, cathedral, and medieval squares taking center stage in most tourists' itineraries. The west is the more modern side, though you'll still find a fair share of Austro-Hungarian architecture; a lot of the city's museums and galleries, as well as the University of Ljubljana, make their home on the western side. The two sides are linked by four bridges, three of which are architecturally interesting (the Zmajski Most, Tromostovje, and Čevljarski Most).

Further west you'll find the beautiful green spaces of Tivoli Gardens, while walking south along the left bank of the Ljubljanica River will land you in the Krakovo district.

Sights

PREŠERNOV TRG
Prešeren Square

This is the place where all of Ljubljana seems to literally meet, from the intersecting city streets to the groups of students on the stairs leading up to the rose-colored **Franciskanska cerkev** (Franciscan Church of the Annunciation, Prešernov trg 4, 8 A.M.–6 P.M. daily, free), Prešernov trg's most striking feature. Inside the mid-17th-century church is an ornate Baroque altar by Francesco Robba, an 18th-century Italian sculptor who spent most of his life in Ljubljana. There are several services daily (7, 8, 9, 10, and 11:15 A.M. and 4, 7, and 9 P.M.).

Also on the square is **Centromerkur** (Trubarjeva 1, tel. 01/426-3170), Ljubljana's oldest department store. Though it's not the best place for shopping, the art nouveau building is worth a look for fans of the style, from the impressive wrought-iron entrance topped with a statue of Mercury to the winding staircases within.

But it's the statue in the square, a monument to Prešeren, that's caused the most fuss in Ljubljana's past. The classical nude by Ivan Zajcs and Maks Fabiani was once seen as scandalous for being placed so close to a church.

◖ Tromostovje
Triple Bridge

Inspired by the bridges of Venice, the Tromostovje is a Plečnik design that has become a city trademark. The Ljubljana-transforming architect added two delicate arched bridges on the sides of the original single bridge, creating a unique and practical effect. The central bridge, once called the Hospital Bridge, was built in 1842. Traffic was creating many problems for the busy thoroughfare, so in 1929 Plečnik had the ingenious idea to build the parallel bridges for pedestrians to prevent the original bridge from being destroyed and to route traffic in a

---

THE GREAT POET FRANCE PREŠEREN

France Prešeren is widely considered to be the greatest Slovenian poet of all time and the force that shaped the country's subsequent literature. He was born in 1800 in Vrba; his parents recognized his intelligence and sent him to elementary school in Ribnica at the age of eight. He attended high school in Ljubljana and university in Vienna, where he studied law.

Prešeren had a tragic life, losing (or actually never winning over) his one true love, never marrying the mother of his three children, losing close friends to death, and battling alcoholism. Still, all of this intense emotional upheaval helped create his beautiful, tender poetry.

The great Romanticist poet of Slovenia, Prešeren's image can be found on the Slovenian two-euro coin and Ljubljana's busy Prešernov trg.

PLEČNIK'S LJUBLJANA

It's rare to have a city almost entirely designed (or at least renovated) by one architect. Though that may be an overstatement, there's no doubt about the strong impression Plečnik left on Ljubljana.

An 1895 earthquake left the city badly damaged and left open a door for Ljubljana to re-create and modernize itself, and it was Jože Plečnik who led the way.

Born in Ljubljana in 1872, Plečnik studied with the famous Viennese architect Otto Wagner, working in his office during the 1890s. He completed several structures in Vienna before moving on to Prague, where the Czech president appointed him the chief architect in charge of renovating Prague Castle.

Plečnik returned to Ljubljana in 1921, transforming the city during the 1920s and '30s. He renovated churches and the municipal cemetery, Žale, and built new bridges, waterfronts, buildings, monuments, and parks.

Jože Plečnik died in Ljubljana in 1957.

DISCOVERING THE ARCHITECT IN A DAY

Start your tour in the Trnovo neighborhood at **Plečnik's house** (Karunova 4, tel. 01/280-1600, www.aml.si, reserve a tour in advance by phone, €4). Today the surprisingly sparse space, preserved as he left it upon his death, gives you a sense of the architect and the man. Cross the **Trnovo Bridge,** with its interesting pyramids mimicking the spires of the Church of St. John the Baptist and the trees growing along the bridge, also a Plečnik idea.

Continue toward the city center on Emonska cesta, stopping at its intersection with Mirje, where even a set of old **Roman walls** were not left untouched by the architect. The most striking of his additions is the large pyramid over one of the openings in the wall.

Back on Emonska, you'll pass the **Faculty of Architecture,** where he taught from 1945 to 1947, and a **monument** to the Illyrians he designed on Trg Francoske Revolucije.

The nearby **Križanke theater** was not only designed by Plečnik (when he was in his eighties, no less), it was also the site of a couple of jokes on the communists who commissioned him to create it. In one of the complex's courtyards he put in a vast amount of lighting, so much that some people questioned the idea. His excuse? The communists needed enlightening. He also placed columns decorated with the hammer and sickle directly opposite a statue of Christ in the main courtyard. Plečnik was a devout Catholic and likely this was his own way of injecting a snub at the Yugoslavian regime.

From here, double back to **Vegova cesta,** a beautiful street planned by the architect. Heading past **Kongresni trg,** which was also touched by Plečnik's skilled hand, though many features have been paved over with asphalt, to the west of the square you'll find a staircase leading to the beautiful tree-lined river **promenade.** From the river, you can see the rear facade of the **Philharmonica,** another Plečnik creation.

Walking along the river, you should hit the **Tromostovje,** or Triple Bridge. It was Plečnik who had the brilliant idea of adding two pedestrian bridges alongside the motor bridge, along with some handsome street lamps. From here, it's off to the **market,** where even the banality of buying bread did not escape his elegant and symmetrical touch.

LJUBLJANA DRAGON

the Ljubljana dragon, a symbol of the city

Dragons don't really figure into much of the architecture around Slovenia and neighboring Croatia, yet the mythical creature holds an important spot in Ljubljana culture. The origins of the Ljubljana dragon are tied closely with Greek legends. The hero who stole the Golden Fleece, Jason, was running away from the king he took it from and was forced to head up the Danube River. From there he and his men sailed to the Sava and then to the Ljubljanica River. On their journey they came across a big lake and marsh, where Jason supposedly fought and killed a vicious monster. The monster, the Ljubljana dragon, remained local folklore and was adopted as a part of Ljubljana's coat of arms and as mascot of the city.

more efficient manner. The balustrade-lined Tromostovje, along with the Zmajski Most, is considered a symbol of the city by locals.

EAST OF PREŠERNOV TRG
Hiša Eksperimentov
House of Experiments

If you're traveling with the kids, check out Hiša Eksperimentov (Trubarjeva 39, tel. 01/300-6888, www.h-e.si, 11 A.M.–7 P.M. Sat.–Sun., €5), a small museum with plenty of hands-on displays teaching scientific principles. Exhibits include a giant bubble maker and a piano that plays music according to weight.

Slovenski Etnografski muzej
Slovene Ethnographic Museum

Though it's a bit out of the way (across the river to the northeast), the Etnografski muzej (Metelkova 2, tel. 01/300-8700, www.etno-muzej.si, 10 A.M.–6 P.M. Tues.–Sun., €4.50) has a good overview of Slovenian cultural history with a look at everything from costumes to folk music. The museum has careful translations in English, making it a more worthwhile stop.

VODNIKOV TRG
Vodnik Square

This attractive square, built at the very end of the 19th century after the earthquake, is home to Ljubljana's central market, filled with colorful stands of fruits and vegetables from Monday through Saturday.

◀ Zmajski Most
Dragon Bridge

It's impossible to miss Zmajski Most, located near Vodnikov trg. It was the first modern bridge to cross the Ljubljanica, and traffic still uses it today. Built in 1901 by Dalmatian architect Jurij Zaninović, it was originally dedicated to Emperor Franz Joseph, but the menacing green dragon statues were just too iconic for the name to catch on. Legend has it that if a virgin walks across the bridge, one of the dragons will wave its tail. A wonderful example of art nouveau architecture, the bridge is mainly important as a symbol of Ljubljana.

Glavna tržnica
Main Market

A trip to the Glavna tržnica (Mon.–Sat. mornings) is a nice break from museums and monuments. However, it's also an essential stop for fans of Plečnik—he designed the market, filled with his signature columns, that stretches

the city's main market

through Pogačarjev trg and Vodnikov trg next to the Cathedral of St. Nicholas.

◖ Stolnica sveti Nikolaja
Cathedral of St. Nicholas

A 1701 Baroque cathedral built on the site of an earlier 13th-century church of the same name, the grand Stolnica sveti Nikolaja (Dolničarjeva 1, tel. 01/234-2690, www.lj-stolnica.rkc.si, 6 A.M.–noon and 3–7 P.M. daily, free) was designed by Italian architect Andrea Pozzo. Inside, there are some pretty frescoes by Quaglio (18th century) and Langus (19th century). Perhaps the biggest don't-miss here, though, are the impressive and solemn **bronze doors,** added in 1996 by artist Tone Demšar to commemorate the Pope's visit and the 1,250th year of Christianity in Slovenia.

Lutkovno Gledališče
Puppet Theater

It's fun to catch a show at the Lutkovno Gledališče (Krekov trg 2, tel. 01/300-0970, www.lgl.si, ticket office 4–6 P.M. Mon.–Fri., 10 A.M.–noon Sat.). If you can't make a show, catch the puppets that pop out of the **clock** above the theater at the top of every hour 8 A.M.–8 P.M.

◖ LJUBLJANSKI GRAD
Ljubljana Castle

The hill that Ljubljanski Grad (Studentovska ulica, reached via Vodnikov trg, tel. 01/432-7216, 9 A.M.–11 P.M. daily Apr.–Oct., 10 A.M.–7 P.M. daily Nov.–Mar., tours at 10 A.M. and 4 P.M. June–mid-Sept., €5) sits on has always been home to forts, first occupied by the Celts, then the Illyrians, and later the Romans. The earliest part of the current structure, however, dates from the early 16th century. The highlights of the castle are the 15th-century **Kapela sv. Jurija** (St. George's Chapel), decorated with 60 colorful coats of arms from the 18th century, and the 19th-century **Lookout Tower,** where you can get a super view of Ljubljana and the Julian Alps. The castle complex has a decent gift shop and a **café** (9 A.M.–11 P.M. daily in summer, 10 A.M.–9 P.M. daily in winter) for a caffeine fix. After your tour, make sure to take time to hike around some of the leafy peaceful paths at the castle's base; the paths were designed by Plečnik in the 1930s.

OLD TOWN

The old core of Ljubljana has a storybook quality, with meticulous Baroque and medieval buildings filled with locals shopping in the small boutiques and stopping for a coffee in the area's many cafés.

Mestna hiša
Town Hall

Built in the 15th century, the imposing Mestna hiša assumed its current appearance during an 18th-century renovation. The best feature of the building is its beautiful Gothic courtyard with a Francisco Robba fountain depicting Narcissus.

Mestni trg
Town Square

It's worth wandering around the small galleries and boutiques on this picturesque cobbled square. The jaunty Baroque facades that line the square replaced the 12th-century square's medieval buildings, most of which were destroyed in the earthquake of 1511. Francesco Robba took his inspiration for **Robbov Vodnjak** (Robba's Fountain, Mestni trg) from fountains he saw while visiting Rome. Built in the 18th century and Robba's final work in Ljubljana before moving to Zagreb, it represents the three rivers of Carniola (Ljubljanica, Sava, and Krka).

From here head down to nearby Ribji trg, the location of Ljubljana's **oldest house** (No. 6), built in 1528.

◖ Gornji trg
Upper Square

Gornji trg is where you'll find the city's **medieval houses** (though the facades are mostly Baroque) and the 17th-century **Cerkev sv. Florijana** (Church of St. Florian, Gornji trg 18, tel. 01/252-1727). The church was built in the late 17th century, though Plečnik left his mark here too when he moved a statue by

Ljubljana's old town

Francesco Robba in front of what was once the main portal.

Flowing out of Gornji trg is **Levstikov trg** (Levstik Square), redesigned in the 20th century (again by Plečnik). It's worth a peek in the Baroque interior of the **Cerkev sv. Jakoba** (Church of St. James, Gornji trg 18, tel. 01/252-1727, services at 8 A.M., 9:15 A.M., 10:30 A.M., and 5 P.M., free), whose 17th-century **Kapela sv. Frančiška Ksaverija** (Chapel of St. Francis Xavier) is probably the prettiest and most ornate church in town. Just across from the church is the rococo **Grubereva Palača** (Gruber Palace, Zvezdarska ulica 1, tel. 01/241-4200), built between 1771 and 1783, which today houses the **Narodni arhiv Slovenije** (National Archives).

Čevljarski Most
Cobblers' Bridge

More of a square than a bridge, this column-lined Plečnik-designed pedestrian bridge divides Gornji trg and Mestni trg, or the old and new sides of town. Though the cobblers' huts that once lined a medieval wooden bridge here are now gone, the name keeps their memory alive.

LEFT BANK

Though it's more modern than the Old Town that skims the base of the castle, Ljubljana's Left Bank is filled with plenty of attractive Austro-Hungarian architecture, as well as many of the city's museums, theaters, and restaurants.

Slovenska Filharmonija
Slovenian Philharmonic Hall

The Slovenska Filharmonija (Kongresni trg 10, tel. 01/241-0800, www.filharmonija.si) is one of the world's older philharmonic orchestras. Originally founded in 1701, its members have included greats such as Haydn, Brahms, and Beethoven. The building was designed by Austrian architect Adolf Wagner and built in 1891. However, even this building did not escape Plečnik's master hand, changing the back facade and adding onto the neo-Renaissance structure.

Moderna galerija
Modern Gallery

The austere, gray home of the Moderna galerija (Tomšičeva 14, tel. 01/241-6800, www.mg-lj.si) is currently closed for extensive renovations. They hope to finish renovation in 2009 to show off the nice collection of contemporary Slovenian art.

Mestni muzej Ljubljana
Ljubljana City Museum

Ljubljana is packed with excellent museums, though the top of your list should be the Mestni muzej Ljubljana (Gosposka 15, tel. 01/241-2500, www.mm-lj.si, 10 A.M.–6 P.M. Tues.–Sun., English guided tours at 1 P.M. Sun., €4), where you can get a quick overview of the city's history, including photographs, documents, and scale models of planned but never completed Plečnik designs.

Narodna galerija
National Gallery

The location of the Narodna galerija (Prešernova 24, tel. 01/241-5418, www.ng-slo.si, 10 A.M.–6 P.M. Tues.–Sun., €5, free Sat. 2–6 P.M.) is worth a visit in itself. The 1896 Czech-designed building is loaded with gilt and over-the-top ceilings, a superb example of the Secessionist era, that lend added grandeur to the fine art housed here. The core of the collection centers on Slovenian art from the 13th to the 20th century, though it also houses a solid collection of European paintings as well. The gallery has a café and a nice shop for souvenirs.

Narodni muzej
National Museum

Though it's the oldest museum in Slovenia, the exhibition at the Narodni muzej (Prešernova 20, tel. 01/241-4400, www.narmuz-lj.si, €3) is relatively small. It features some Roman stone monuments, an Egyptian mummy, bronze artifacts from the Illyrians, and various artifacts, weapons, jewelry, and archaeological finds.

Železniški muzej
Railway Museum

Young and old should enjoy the Železniški

muzej (Parmova 35, tel. 01/291-2641, 10 A.M.–6 P.M. Tues.–Sun., €3). Admire the shiny steam engines, railway memorabilia, uniforms, and even art from Slovenia's history of railroading. You'll also find some decaying trains in the yard outside and a re-creation of a station master's office inside.

Pivovarski muzej
Brewery Museum
Fans of beer or history or both will appreciate the charming Pivovarski muzej (Pivovarniška 2, tel. 01/471-7340, www.pivo-union.si, 8 A.M.–1 P.M. first Tues. of the month, reserve in advance, free). Located in the 150-year-old Union Brewery, the displays consist of the history of brewing in Slovenia, a tour of the brewery, and a beer tasting.

Tobačni muzej
Tobacco Museum
Though it may not be politically correct, the Tobačni muzej (Tobačna 5, tel. 01/477-7344, www.tobacna.si, 10 A.M.–6 P.M. first Wed. and third Thurs. of the month, free) is quite interesting even for non-smokers. Not only do the displays track tobacco's history in Europe since the Middle Ages, but it also shows the importance of the factory for women's emancipation in Slovenia.

TIVOLI PARK
A giant peaceful green space in the middle of the city, Tivoli Park is so big it makes one think previous generations had very high hopes for Ljubljana's growth. A Plečnik-landscaped promenade leads to the **Tivoli Mansion,** where the **Mednarodni Grafični Likovni Center** (International Center for Graphic Arts, Pod Turnom 3, tel. 01/241-3800, www.mglc-lj.si, 11 A.M.–6 P.M. Wed.–Sun., €3.50) resides today. The center is a must for fans of graphic and visual arts, with posters, book designs, and more, most from the second half of the 20th century. Children will like the small zoo, while history fans will like the **Muzej Novejše Zgodovine** (Museum of Modern History, Celovška 23, tel. 01/300-9610, www.muzej-nz.si, 10 A.M.–6 P.M. Tues.–Sun., €3.50), where an excellent display of Slovenian history during the 20th century will leave you feeling like you know the country a little better than before.

KRAKOVO
A pleasant neighborhood to walk around, dating from the 15th century, Krakovo was originally a fishermen's settlement and later home to the Slovenian impressionist painter Rihard Jakopič; the neighborhood still has an organic, almost country feel to it. The **Jakopič Garden** (Mirje 4, tel. 01/241-2506, www.mm-lj.si, dawn–dusk) is home to a few Roman ruins, including a few additions to the ancient walls by Plečnik, but the real draw to Krakovo is its artsy, unpretentious vibe. Wander the enclave of peasant-style homes, many with gardens that supply the town market, and narrow little streets with pleasing flower and vegetable patches, and stop at one of the funky cafés.

Entertainment and Events

NIGHTLIFE
Bars

Ljubljana has a great bar and club scene with something for everyone. Literary and artsy types might want to check out the **KUD France Prešeren** (Karunova 14, tel. 01/283-2288, 11 A.M.–1 A.M. daily), home to a small café and a strong presence on Ljubljana's arts scene since 1919. Something happens here most every night, from readings and performances to concerts and workshops. **Geonatvik** (Kongresni trg 1, tel. 01/252-7027, www.geonavtik.com, 7 A.M.–1 A.M. Mon.–Thurs., 7 A.M.–3 A.M. Fri., 8:30 A.M.–3 A.M. Sat.) is a café/shop selling maps and guides that also hosts the odd travel lecture or live music act, advertised on the chalkboard out front. Relatively undiscovered, the just-out-of-center **Pilon** (Prešernova 15) is aesthetically pleasing, plus it has lots of artsy and style-conscious magazines to peruse if you're bored. The interior of **Boheme** (Mestni trg 19, tel. 01/548-1342) often gets overlooked by patrons, but the shabby elegance lends one to literary musings.

Trendy sorts and fashionistas should check out **Salon** (Trubarjeva 23, tel. 01/439-8764, www.salon.si, 9 A.M.–1 A.M. Mon.–Wed., 9 A.M.–3 A.M. Thurs.–Sat., 3 P.M.–1 A.M. Sun.) where kitsch decor competes with the trendily dressed crowd, downing some quite good cocktails. **Kuriln'ca** (Mestni trg 18) has a more serious interior and is definitely part of the popular crowd. The decor at **Minimal** (Mestni trg 4, tel. 01/426-0138) is supplied by the well-dressed patrons. The bar has a good drinks list and sushi on Wednesday night.

Maček (Krojaška 5, tel. 01/425-3791, 9 A.M.–midnight daily) is in the heart of Ljubljana's hip right bank. A prime people-watching spot, it's a popular place for weekend morning coffee.

A more professional, albeit chic, crowd swill coffee by day and cocktails by night at the attractive **Opera Bar** (Cankarjeva 12, tel. 01/421-0390, www.opera-bar.com, 7 A.M.–12:30 A.M. Mon.–Wed., 7 A.M.–2 A.M. Thurs.–Sat., 10 A.M.–6 P.M. Sun.).

Beer lovers fear not: Ljubljana has dozens of pubs to choose from. Narrowing down the list, try **Zlata Ladjica** (Jurčičev trg 1, tel. 01/241-0696, www.zlataladjica.si, 8 A.M.–1 A.M. Mon.–Sat., 10 A.M.–10 P.M. Sun.), where riverside outdoor seating and great old-town views are the draw, or **Kratochwill** (Kolodvorska 14, tel. 01/433-3114, www.kratochwill.si, 9 A.M.–11 P.M. Mon.–Fri., noon–11 P.M. Sat., noon–10 P.M. Sun.), the city's only microbrewery, for local flavor. If you're feeling homesick, try expat hangouts **Cutty Sark** (Knafjlev prehod 1, tel. 01/425-1477, 9 A.M.–1 A.M. Mon.–Sat., noon–1 A.M. Sun.) or **Patrick's** (Prečna 6, tel. 01/230-1768, 10 A.M.–1 A.M. Mon.–Fri., noon–1 A.M. Sat., 5 P.M.–midnight Sun.) for on-tap Guinness and English-speaking companionship. Sports fans will like the gimmicky **Rugby Pub & Lounge** (Židovska Steza 6, tel. 01/426-4062, 8 A.M.–12:30 A.M. Mon.–Thurs., 8 A.M.–1 A.M. Fri., noon–1 A.M. Sat., noon–midnight Sun.) for three floors of big-screen TVs blaring sporting events, lots of beer, and sport-themed decoration.

Students shouldn't miss **Zmavc** (Rimska 21, tel. 01/251-0324, 7:30 A.M.–1 A.M. Mon.–Fri., 10 A.M.–1 A.M. Sat., 6 P.M.–1 A.M. Sun.), a graffiti-covered bar filled with comic-strip walls, raucous fun-loving staff and customers, and a general good vibe. Also worth checking out: **Birdland** (Trubarjeva 50, tel. 01/231-7937, 1 P.M.–midnight Mon.–Fri., 4 P.M.–midnight Sat.–Sun.) for a friendly, laid-back spot with few patrons over 25. Art and philosophy majors will appreciate **NUK café** (Turjaška 1), in the basement of the stunning National University Library, which affords lots of private nooks for deep discussions.

If you're in the mood for something different, Slovenia's capital has lots of theme bars, from the skeleton-filled **Pr Skelet** (Ključavničarska 5, tel. 01/252-7799, 10 A.M.–3 A.M. daily) cocktail bar to Hemingway memorial **Casa del**

Papa (Celovška 54, tel. 01/434-3158, noon–midnight daily), which plays pop music instead of something more atmospheric, but the drinks make up for the faux pas. If you're feeling a bit juvenile, race electric go-karts around a track at the racing-themed **Rollbar** (Hala 18, tel. 01/585-2570, www.indoor-karting.com, 7 A.M.–midnight Mon.–Thurs., 8 A.M.–1:30 A.M. Fri.–Sat., 8 A.M.–11 P.M. Sun.) in the BTC City shopping center.

If all the bars have closed and you want to keep going, join the after party at rowdy Turbo-Folk **Klub 12** (Prušnikova 95, tel. 041/678-577, www.klub-12.com, 7 A.M.–5 A.M. Mon.–Fri., 6 P.M.–5 A.M. Sat.–Sun.) or the faithful **Druga Pomoč** (Šmartinska 3, tel. 01/431-3277, 6 A.M.–3 A.M. daily), serving drinks with a smile to the bleary-eyed hardcore.

Live Music and Dance Clubs

A solid choice for chilling out to a quality jam session, the elegant but low-key **Gajo Jazz Club** (Beethovnova 8, tel. 01/425-3206, www.jazzclubgajo.com, 9 A.M.–1 A.M. Mon.–Fri., 9 A.M.–midnight Sat.–Sun.) hosts local and international acts. For more party atmosphere with your jazz, **Sax Pub** (Eipporva 7, tel. 01/283-1457, 10 A.M.–1 A.M. Tues.–Sat., 4–10 P.M. Sun., noon–1 A.M. Mon.) has Thursday-night live jazz inside a graffiti-painted riverside cottage.

Students should head to **KMŠ** (Tržaška 2, tel. 01/425-7480, www.klubkms.si, 8 A.M.–5 A.M. Mon.–Fri., 9 P.M.–5 A.M. Sat.), a student-run club located in an old factory. Inside, two floors host a young crowd that fills to capacity on weekends.

Klub K4 (Kersnikova 4, tel. 01/438-0261, www.k4.org, from 11 P.M. Tues.–Sun.) is a Ljubljana club-scene establishment, with a nondescript metal and neon interior and something different every night, ranging from techno to funk to Sunday's pink party for the local gay community.

Aspiring supermodels line up in front of **Global** (Tomšičeva 1, tel. 01/426-9020, www.global.si, 9 A.M.–5 A.M. Mon.–Sat.) to mix with the in crowd and enjoy great views of the city from atop the Nama department store.

On the more extreme side (or at least as extreme as Ljubljana gets) **Metelkovo Mesto** (Metelkova cesta, tel. 01/432-3378, www.metelkova.org, call or visit website for schedule) is a former army barracks that hosts themed events, including punk, dance, and gay/lesbian. It's usually hard to find out what's

---

TURBO-FOLK

Hundreds of kids stand on tables, arms around each other, loudly belting out the lyrics of a Turbo-Folk song on a Saturday night. It sounds whiny and very – well, Balkan, which is not a word most Croatians or Slovenians like to be associated with.

More importantly, Turbo-Folk is almost strictly Serbian, and for many older Croatians (and Slovenians as well) who still remember the scars of the war, the idea of embracing a part of Serbian culture seems traitorous. The topic has created a lot of debate in Croatia, from radio talk shows to political television interviews with calls for banning the music, which is not played on television or local radio stations.

Locally referred to as *narodnjaci* (closest translation: folk music), it was described by a journalist from Croatia's *Jutarnji List* newspaper as "a mixture of mutated Balkan melodies, howling vocals, idiotic lyrics and sampled disco and house rhythms." Think of something like country music, with its themes of lost love, adultery, and revenge, mixed with gangsta rap's big cars, big guns, and big money, and you'd have something close to Turbo-Folk.

The controversy is somewhat less in Slovenia, and if you'd like to get a taste, Ljubljana is a safer place to do it than Croatia, where the underground Turbo-Folk scene often gets mixed in with other underground pursuits and unsavory groups under the influence of too much alcohol.

going on ahead of time, so if you can't get anyone on the phone, have a peek to see if it seems like your style.

Packed, sweaty, and loud are a few words you could use to describe **Orto Bar** (Grablovičeva 1, tel. 01/232-1674, 8 P.M.–4 A.M. daily), a lounge swathed in red velvet serving shots and pulsing music from blues to punk.

THE ARTS

Ljubljanski Grad (Ljubljana Castle, Studentovska ulica, tel. 01/232-9994, www.ljubljanafestival.si) hosts musical and theatrical performances throughout the year. **Poletno gledališče Križank** (Križanke Summer Theater, Miklošičeva 28, tel. 01/439-6445, www.ljubljanafestival.si) is an open-air theater located on the site of a former monastery. The entire complex has a sliding roof that makes for outstanding theater and concerts, from classical to pop and jazz, in all sorts of weather. Home to the Slovenian Philharmonic Orchestra, the **Slovenska Filharmonija,** the Philharmonic Hall (Kongresni trg, tel. 01/241-0800, www.filharmonija.si) is a dependable venue for solid classical performances. The frothy 1882 home of the **Slovensko narodno gledališče** (Slovenian National Opera and Ballet Theater, Zupančičeva 1, tel. 01/425-4840) is a fitting location for Verdi, Mozart, and *Swan Lake.* If you're traveling with kids or you're just a kid at heart, a marionette show at the **Lutkovno Gledališče** (Puppet Theater, Krekov trg 2, tel. 01/300-0970, www.lgl.si, ticket office 4–6 P.M. Mon.–Fri., 10 A.M.–noon Sat.) is a nice way to while away an afternoon.

No need to hunt for a special foreign-language cinema in Slovenia. Most films (with the exception of some children's films) are not dubbed, only subtitled, which means you can easily rub shoulders with the locals and still enjoy the movie. Try the old-school but renovated **Kinoklub Vič** (Trg Mladinskih Delovnih Brigad 6, tel. 01/241-8411, www.kolosej.si) for major releases and the occasional offbeat movie. For art and foreign films (fun if you speak French, less choice if you only speak

Ljubljana Jazz Festival

English), check out **Kinoteka** (Miklošičeva 28, tel. 01/547-1580, www.kinoteka.si). For the standard big multiplex experience, head to BTC City, where **Kolosej** (Šmartinska 152, tel. 01/520-5500, www.kolosej.si) has a big selection of Hollywood blockbusters.

FESTIVALS AND EVENTS

The **Festival Dokumentarnega Filma** (International Festival of Documentary Film, www.fdf.si) screens documentary films from around the world every year in late March or early April. At the beginning of May, the **Wire Walk** (www.pohod.si), whose longest trek is 35 kilometers around the city, memorializes Ljubljana's occupation by the Italians who surrounded the city with barbed wire during World War II.

Museums are free of charge on the International Day of Museums (May 18), the Museum Summer Night (usually June 16), and the Day of Culture (Dec. 3), celebrating the birthday of Prešeren.

The **Ljubljana Festival** (www.ljubljanafestival.si), held every summer from sometime in June to sometime in August, is an outstanding arts festival that brings together international chamber and symphony orchestras, visual artists, and even an open-air cinema for dozens of cultural performances. Summer also brings the **Ljubljana Jazz Festival** (www.ljubljanajazz.si), an outstanding event that has been an annual feature for 50 years. **Trnfest** is another summer festival, bringing free concerts and performances to the Trnovo neighborhood the entire month of August.

In December, Christmas spirit fills Ljubljana's streets, with decorations and lots of stalls selling gifts and refreshments in the Old Town.

Shopping and Recreation

SHOPPING
English Books

If you are really interested in the local topography or are looking for detailed city maps, the best store is **Kod in kam** (Trg francoske revolucije 7, tel. 01/200-2732, 9 A.M.–8 P.M. Mon.–Fri., 8 A.M.–1 P.M. Sat.), located near the National University Library. For reprints of classics in English, maps, and dictionaries, head to **Oxford Center** (Kopitarjeva 2, tel. 01/360-3789, 8 A.M.–7 P.M. Mon.–Fri., 8 A.M.–1 P.M. Sat.), which stocks a large supply of titles for locals learning English. The downtown location of **Konzorcij** (Slovenska 29, tel. 01/241-0650, 9 A.M.–7:30 P.M. Mon.–Fri., 9 A.M.–1 P.M. Sat.) has a nice supply of foreign-language titles, including travel, and it has free Wi-Fi. The cheapest deal in town is the underground **Bukvarna** (across from the Ursuline church on Slovenska, 10 A.M.–1 P.M. and 3–6 P.M. Tues. and Thurs.), which stocks used Slovenian books and a good selection of secondhand English books, priced by weight.

Food and Wine

If you'd like to pick up some souvenirs for the gourmets in your life, the wine shop of **Koželj** (Dvorni trg 1, tel. 01/251-3644, www.kozelj.si, 11 A.M.–8 P.M. Mon.–Fri., 10 A.M.–2 P.M. Sat.) is a must on your shopping trip. Around 80 percent of its selection is local and it's a great place to find out all you ever wanted to know about Slovenian winemaking. **Čokoladnica Cukrček** (Mestni trg 11, tel. 01/519-9286, www.cukrcek.si, 9 A.M.–8 P.M. Mon.–Sat., 10 A.M.–7 P.M. Sun.) has hundreds of attractively packaged chocolate confections, hot chocolates, and even chocolates shaped like Ljubljana's signature dragon or one of its most famous poets, Prešeren. You also may want to pop by the **Glavna tržnica** (Main Market, tel. 01/300-1200, Mon.–Sat. mornings) for locally produced honeys and other sundries.

Foodies will also appreciate the stash at **Honey House** (Mestni trg 7, 10 A.M.–6 P.M. Mon.–Fri., 10 A.M.–1 P.M. Sat.), with everything you could imagine produced from honey, including wine and candies. **Piranske soline** (Mestni trg 19, tel. 01/425-0190, 9 A.M.–8 P.M. Mon.–Fri., 9 A.M.–5 P.M. Sat., 10 A.M.–3 P.M. Sun.) sells a range of products from bath salts to cooking salts, all from the famous salt pans of the coastal city of Piran. Don't pass up trying the salted chocolates.

Souvenirs

You can buy lace from Idrija, whose long tradition of lace-making is legendary in Slovenia, at **Idrijska čipka** (Mestni trg 17, tel. 01/425-0051, www.idrija-lace.com, 10 A.M.–1 P.M. and 3–7 P.M. Mon.–Fri.). Though much of it is typical souvenir bric-a-brac, you might find something for your suitcase at **Rustika** (Ljubljana Castle, Studentovska ulica, 9 A.M.–8 P.M. daily in summer, 10 A.M.–7 P.M. daily in winter) inside Ljubljana Castle.

Antiques

The riverside **Sunday market** (Cankarjevo Nabrežje, 8 A.M.–2 P.M. Sun.) near the Cobblers' Bridge is the place to find fun antiques, old postcards, and jewelry to stash in your suitcase. For antiques of a different sort, **Spin Vinyl Rock n Roll Ploščarna** (Gallusovo Nabrežje 13, tel. 01/251-1018, 10 A.M.–7 P.M. Mon.–Fri., 10:30 A.M.–2 P.M. Sat.) is an old-school old-town record shop selling stacks of vinyl from the former Yugoslavia—a fun souvenir for music fans.

Fashion

Though avant-garde knitting might seem like an oxymoron, **Draž** (Gornji trg 9, tel. 01/426-6041, www.drazdraz.com, tel. 01/426-6041, 9 A.M.–1 P.M. and 3–7 P.M. Mon.–Fri., 10 A.M.–1 P.M. Sat.) just might change your mind. The local fashion house designs dresses, skirts, and sweaters that are all runway ready.

Shopping Centers

If you still haven't found quite what you're looking for, **BTC City** (Šmartinska 152, tel. 01/585-1100, www.btc-city.com, 9 A.M.–9 P.M. Mon.–Sat.), a few kilometers northeast of the center, has 400 shops, restaurants, bars, a cinema, a post-office, and even a water park.

SPORTS AND RECREATION
City Tours

Ljubljana offers several excellent tours, including a two-hour **walking tour** (depart from the town hall, check with tourist office for times, €10) of the Old Town and castle complex, one-hour **boat tour** (depart from the Cankarjevo nabrežje dock, check with tourist office for times, €10), and two-hour guided **bike tour** (check with tourist office for times and departure points, May–Oct., €20).

Recreation

The **Pot spominov in tovarništva** (Path of Remembrance and Comradeship, www.pohod.si) is a 35-kilometer circuit commemorating the Italian occupation during World War II, following the perimeter that was enclosed in barbed wire. Today, it's a great trek or cycling path through the city's surroundings, passing some worthwhile stops like Plečnik's re-creation of the municipal graveyard, Žale cemetery, and Fužine castle. Follow the signs marked POT.

Skok Sport Center (Marinovseva 8, tel. 01/512-4402, www.skok-sport.si) offers rafting, kayaking, and cycling, as well as kayaking courses around Ljubljana and beyond. The center also rents bicycles and canoes. If you'd like to take to the skies, **Balonarski Center Barje** (Flandrova 1, tel. 01/512-9220, balon@siolnet) or the tourist office can help arrange balloon flights over the city and countryside.

Spectator Sports

Ljubljana's soccer team plays at **ŽSD Stadium** (Milčinskega ulica 2, tel. 01/438-6470). One of the most popular spectator sports these days is hockey; the Ljubljana team HDD Tilia Olimpija takes to the ice at **Hala Tivoli** (Tivoli Hall, Celovška cesta 25, tel. 01/431-5155). The sports hall is also home to basketball and volleyball games. A great source of tickets in Ljubljana, for both sporting events and concerts, is www.eventim.si.

Accommodations

Ljubljana is quite expensive in terms of accommodation, particularly when it comes to value for money. But there are a few gems, and the city has an impressive range of hostel accommodations, some of which seem more like hotels than the backpacker establishments they claim to be. Hotels and guesthouses can be found in the center of town, in the old town core and around the most-frequented tourist sites, as well as out of center, so be sure to figure in time and transportation costs when deciding between your options.

CENTRAL
Under €50

The **Hostel Simbol Castle** (Gerbičeva ulica 46, tel. 041/720-825, www.simbol.si, €15 per person) is in the city center, walking distance to most tourist stops and the train and bus stations. The **Most Hostel** (Petkovškovo nabrežje 41, tel. 041/632-800, €30 d.) exceeds hostel expectations, with a whirlpool tub and shower, fast free Internet, and friendly staff, all a mere five-minute walk to the Dragon Bridge.

The **Hostel Celica** (Metelkova Ulica 8, tel. 01/230-9700, www.hostelcelica.com, €25 per person) is by far one of the most interesting hostels anywhere. Located in a former military prison, most of the rooms are actually cells, all immaculately clean. The mood here is student-party central, with free Internet; it's very close to the train station and ten minutes' walk to the center of town.

€50-100

The **Bed and Breakfast Petra Varl** (Vodnikov trg 5a, tel. 01/430-3788, petra@varl.si, €60 d., including breakfast) is a charming little bed-and-breakfast, a two-minute stroll from the center, with friendly service from the artist-owner. The room with the terrace is particularly sweet.

Certainly one of the best places to stay in Ljubljana, the **C Slamic Bed & Breakfast** (Kersnikova Ulica 1, tel. 01/433-8213, www.slamic.si, €95 d., including breakfast) offers surprisingly luxe rooms, complete with cable TV, free Internet access, and hardwood floors. Located only 10 minutes' walk to either the train and bus stations or the Old Town core, the small hotel also has a popular (and very good) café and sweet shop on the ground floor, perfect for a leisurely breakfast before sightseeing.

If you're interested in **private apartments** in town (a great value for families or for those that like to prepare their own meals), clean and cozy flats are available from www.apartmaji.si.

Over €100

The **Antiq Hotel** (Gornji trg 3, tel. 01/421-3560, www.antiqhotel.si, €144 d., including breakfast) has an excellent location on a pedestrian square in the center of town. The hotel's decor is either homey (lace-trimmed towels and antique furniture) or outdated grandmotherly, depending on your attitude. The only downside for some travelers might be the stairs—the building has no elevator.

With all the amenities of big chain hotels, such as an in-hotel sauna, restaurant, lounge bar, and valet parking, the **Best Western Hotel Slon** (Slovenska cesta 34, tel. 01/470-1100, www.hotelslon.com, €190 d., including breakfast) has swank public spaces in a restored 1930s-era building. The rooms don't have the same character but the hotel is convenient, a short walk to the old town, and has free Internet access in the lobby.

While it's hard to see all five of the stars the **Lev Hotel** (Vošnjakova ulica 1, tel. 01/433-2155, www.hotel-lev.si, €195 d., including breakfast) advertises, its location on the edge of Tivoli Gardens is nice and it's clean and comfortable with free parking, a restaurant, and a bar all on-site.

The **Grand Hotel Union Executive** (Miklošičeva 1, tel. 01/308-1270, www.gh-union.si, €230 d.) has a perfect location in the center of old Ljubljana and a pool for those who'd like to take a dip. The hotel has a stunning art nouveau facade and while the rooms are quite nice, their basic hotel-standard interiors don't live up to the promising entrance.

OUT OF THE CENTER
Under €50

If you happen to be in Ljubljana during the summer, the cheapest accommodations around are the *dijaški dom* (contact the tourist office at the Triple Bridge, €15 d.), or student dorms. All are well connected by bus, with stops located conveniently next to the dorms; they are also walkable, from 10 to 30 minutes from the center. The rooms are simply furnished, with one to three single beds, and it's hard to beat the price.

€50-100

A guesthouse option is **Pri Zabarju** (Viška cesta, tel. 01/428-2462, www.prizabarju.si, €90 d., including breakfast), a cozy place with air-conditioning, parking, a restaurant of the same name, and a sinful cake place all in one convenient location. You'll need to take a bus or taxi to get from this spot, approximately four kilometers west of the core, to the center of things.

Over €100

Despite the fact it's located 2.2 kilometers from the city center, the **AHotel** (Cesta Dveh Cesarjev 34D, tel. 01/429-1892, www.ahotel.si, €125 d., including breakfast) is possibly the best value-for-money hotel in town. With a sleek, trendy lobby and bar, sparkling minimalist rooms, and a good continental breakfast buffet, the AHotel isn't exactly luxe, but it still exceeds expectations. It's located in Trnovo, a very pretty old quarter of town, and is well connected by bus.

The **Austria Trend Hotel** (Dunjaska 154, tel. 01/588-2510, www.austria-trend.at/lju, €222 d.) offers sleek and spacious rooms. The hotel is two kilometers north of town in Bežigrad, connected by shuttle or via bus to the city center.

The uber-modern **Mons Hotel** (Pot za Brdom 55, tel. 01/470-2700, www.hotel.mons.si, €195 d.) is a couple of kilometers west of the center. Be aware that sometimes the service does not live up to the hotel's four stars, and be sure to ask for a room facing the woods rather than the highway. There is a free shuttle to the center, or you can take a taxi.

Food

CENTRAL
Breakfast

The immensely popular **Le Petite Café** (Trg francoske revolucije 4, tel. 01/251-2575, 7:30 A.M.–11 P.M. Mon.–Fri., 9 A.M.–11 P.M. Sat.–Sun., €8) is a local pick for breakfast staples (eggs, toasted baguettes) in a Provençal-themed café.

Cafés and Desserts

For ice cream, the unassuming **Pixi** (Mestni trg 17, tel. 01/426-8460) has some great homemade flavors and a few desserts. The often overlooked **Pri Vodnjaku** (Stari trg 30, tel. 01/425-0712, 8 A.M.–midnight daily) has super old-school atmosphere in which to sip tea and tuck into dessert. The park-side **Zvezda** (Wolfova 14, tel. 01/420-9090, 7 A.M.–11 P.M. Mon.–Sat., 10 A.M.–8 P.M. Sun.) is far trendier and offers lots of ice cream, coffees, and cakes, while **Babo Juice Bar** (Krojaška 4, tel. 040/533-334, 9 A.M.–9 P.M. daily) has some 50 juice combos. Located smack in the old town, it's the perfect spot to refuel for some more sightseeing.

For real tea, from English to herbal, served in pretty porcelain for flair, try **Cha** (Stari trg 3, tel. 01/252-7010, 9 A.M.–10.30 P.M. Mon.–Fri., 9 A.M.–3 P.M. and 6–10:30 P.M. Sat.).

Fine Dining

Foodies should head straight to the cozy **Hiša Kulinarke Manna** (Eipprova ul. 1/A, tel. 01/283-5294, www.kulinarika-manna.com, noon–midnight Mon.–Sat., €30) for slow-food specialties like smoked duck breast with horseradish terrine, lamb with herb crust, and the house cake, Manna.

While **Gostilna As** (Čopova 5a, tel. 01/425-8822, www.gostilnaas.si, noon–midnight daily, €25) may not be as trendy as some spots on the city's restaurant scene, it is still the establishment restaurant of Ljubljana's movers and shakers. The food is excellent, the atmosphere warm and local, and the terrace is superb for warm-weather dining.

Špajza (Gornji trg 28, tel. 01/425-3094, noon–11 P.M. Mon.–Sat., €19) has local atmosphere infused with a romantic vibe. Serving typical Slovenian dishes (think horse and venison) prepared with care as well as a good selection of fish, brought in daily from Croatia, the restaurant has a nice outdoor courtyard for fair-weather dining. **Pri Vitezu** (Breg 20, tel. 01/426-6058, noon–11 P.M. Mon.–Sat., €18) is another choice, from the owner of the popular Luka Gourmet. With a focus on seafood from the Adriatic coast, but with plenty of dishes for more beefy palates as well, the food and service live up to the reputation for quality.

International

If you've had enough local flavor for one day and need a Szechuan noodle fix, **nim8min** (Kolodvorska 20, tel. 01/231-2168, 11 A.M.–11 P.M., €4) has delicious, and cheap, hot wok meals served in eight minutes or less.

The name, **Falafel** (Trubarjeva 40, tel. 041/640-166, 10 A.M.–midnight Mon.–Sat., 1–10 P.M. Sun., €4), describes this miniscule spot's menu pretty well. In addition to the Middle Eastern staple, it serves hummus, burgers, and pizza.

Joe Peña's (Cankarjeva 6, tel. 01/421-5800, www.joepenas.si, 10 A.M.–1 A.M. Mon.–Thurs., 10 A.M.–2 A.M. Fri.–Sat., noon–midnight Sun., €9) is quite possibly the best Mexican in the former Yugoslavia. With an impressive array of fajitas, enchiladas, and margaritas, the place can be packed around midday with lunch voucher–wielding students.

Currently (though probably not for long) the only sushi in Ljubljana, **Sushimama** (Wolfova ulica 12, tel. 01/426-9125, 11 A.M.–11 P.M. daily, €12) serves up rolls and sashimi to a trendy, mostly young crowd.

Local Cuisine

It's worth the trouble to find slightly hidden **Operna Klet** (Zupančičeva 2, tel. 01/252-7003, 11 A.M.–11 P.M. Mon.–Fri., 11 A.M.–6 P.M. Sat., €19) for the excellent selection of Adriatic fish, particularly the octopus salad, served in a no-frills but usually packed space.

Pasta and Pizza

Head to the laid-back **Pasta Nona** (Gosposvetska 2, tel. 01/438-2424, 8 A.M.–11 P.M. Mon.–Fri., €8) for big bowls of pasta and tasty salads. Located in the center of the city's business district, it fills to capacity around lunch.

Though the funky restaurant has sometimes less-than-stellar service, **Foculus** (Gregorčičeva 3, tel. 01/251-5643, 10 A.M.–midnight Mon.–Sat., noon–midnight Sun., €7) is a must-visit for fans of pizza, with over 60 varieties, including Turkish, truffle, and seafood.

For breakfast, lunch, or dinner, unassuming **Luka Gourmet** (Stari trg 9, tel. 01/425-0118, www.lunchcafe.net, 9 A.M.–11 P.M. Mon.–Fri., €15) goes beyond just the typical pasta dishes, serving a full menu, mostly Italian inspired, from Caesar salads to truffle steak to Pannacotta. The killer location right on Stari trg combined with the great value-for-money food (order one of the homemade soups) means it may be hard to snag a table, so reservations are recommended.

As Lounge (Čopova 5a, tel. 01/425-8822, www.gostilnaas.si, 9 A.M.–3 A.M. daily, €9) is the more casual offshoot of the pricier Gostilna As. Turning into a popular club spot as the night wears on, it's also the destination for pastas and salads at reasonable prices in a swank setting.

Quick Bites

Ljubljana has a great selection of budget-friendly restaurants aimed at locals on their lunch break and students in need of sustenance. **Paninoteka** (Jurčičev Trg 3, tel. 01/425-0055, 8 A.M.–1 A.M. Mon.–Sat., 9 A.M.–11 P.M. Sun., €4) is the place to go for generous sandwiches made with fresh Italian bread. It's hard to miss the location of **Tramvaj Ekspres Pizzeria** (Trg mladinskih Delovnih Brigad 10, tel. 041/916-407, 10 A.M.–6 P.M. Mon.–Fri., closed mid-July–mid-Aug., €6): two old bright-red trams parked in the center of a city square. Hungry students pack inside to pick up pizza and hot sandwiches.

Tomato (Šubičeva 1, tel. 01/252-7555, www.tomato.si, 7 A.M.–9 P.M. Mon.–Fri., €3) has an extensive menu of breakfast dishes, sandwiches, burgers, and pastas at amazing prices, catering to an exam-cramming crowd. The same students that haunt Tomato by day may be found around **Nobel Burek** (Miklošičeva 30, tel. 01/232-3392, 24 hours, €2) by night. Conveniently located near the bus and train stations, it offers steaming hot *burek* and pizza 24 hours a day.

If you'd prefer to be surrounded by a slightly older, more business-y crowd, try **Restaurant 2000** (Trg Republike 1, tel. 01/476-6925, 7 A.M.–7 P.M. Mon.–Fri., 8 A.M.–5 P.M. Sat., €6) for basic but filling cafeteria food inside Maxi market.

Vegetarian

Technically, the only vegetarian restaurant in town is outside the city center. However, several mainstream restaurants offer a good variety of vegetarian dishes, like **Foculus** (Gregorčičeva 3, tel. 01/251-5643, 10 A.M.–midnight Mon.–Sat., noon–midnight Sun., €7) and **Falafel** (Trubarjeva 40, tel. 041/640-166, 10 A.M.–midnight Mon.–Sat., 1–10 P.M. Sun., €4), both described earlier.

OUT OF THE CENTER
Fine Dining

Though the cuisine is not as haute as the more central Manna, **Gostilna Kaval** (Tacenska 95, tel. 01/512-5596, www.bid.si/kaval, 10 A.M.–11 P.M. Mon.–Fri., noon–11 P.M. Sat.–Sun., €15), about seven kilometers northwest of the center, has some tasty Tuscan-inspired cuisine and a romantic terrace at pretty good prices.

The swank space at **Cubo** (Šmartinska c. 55, tel. 01/521-1515, www.cubo-ljubljana.com, 11 A.M.–11 P.M. Mon.–Fri., noon–11 P.M. Sat., €18), about three kilometers northeast of the center, is as stylish as its food. A Mediterranean-inspired menu and sinful desserts are gobbled up by a chic clientele.

Local Cuisine

Vinske Kleti Slovenija (Dunjaska 18, tel. 01/431-5015, 11 A.M.–11 P.M. Mon.–Fri., 4–11 P.M. Sat., €20) is the country's largest wine shop; the accompanying cellar restaurant is one of the best places to try good Slovenian dishes with one of some 80 local wines. It's about two kilometers north in the Bežigrad neighborhood, not far from the Austria Trend Hotel.

While all its dishes aren't exactly Slovenian, **Gostilna pod Rožnikom** (Cesta na Rožnik 18, tel. 01/251-3436, www.gp-vic.si/roznik.asp, 10 A.M.–11 P.M. Mon.–Fri., noon–11 P.M. Sat.–Sun., €19) has a great selection of regional cuisine, like grilled *ražnjiči* skewers, fried sweet peppers, and Serbian salads. Located in a leafy spot near the city zoo, it also has a huge shady terrace for alfresco dining.

Worth the drive or taxi ride to the edge of town for a special meal, the ◉ **Gostilna Kovač** (Pot k Savi 9, tel. 01/537-1244, www.kovac-co.si, noon–10 P.M. Mon.–Fri., €38) has been serving traditional Slovenian cuisine since 1849. The interior is romantic, with wood-beamed ceilings and antiques, and there's a nice terrace as well. The restaurant is about five kilometers northeast of the center, just above the Bežigrad neighborhood.

Quick Bites

Though many may find it offensive, **Hot Horse** (Tivoli Park, tel. 01/521-1427, www.hothorse.si, 10 A.M.–6 A.M. Mon., 9 A.M.–6 A.M. Tues.–Sun., €3) is a local institution, serving late-night horseburgers next to Tivoli Park. They have a veggie burger on the menu too, though it's doubtful that many animal lovers are eating here.

In the Krakovo district, **Okrepčevapnica** (Vrtna 8, tel. 041/843-106, €8) is the place to go to sample grilled-meat specialties straight from Sarajevo. Wash it down with a Turkish coffee, accompanied by a complimentary cigarette. See a slice of Bosnia without putting the stamp in your passport.

Vegetarian
On the northeastern side of Tivoli Park, **Vegedrom** (Vodnikova 35, tel. 01/513-2642, www.vegedrom.com, 9 A.M.–10 P.M. Mon.–Fri., noon–10 P.M. Sat., €7) serves great vegan and vegetarian dishes, many with an Indian twist.

Information and Services

TOURIST AND TRAVEL INFORMATION

The **Tourist Information Center** (Adamič-Lundrovo Nabrežje 2, tel. 01/306-1215, www.ljubljana-tourism.si, 8 A.M.–9 P.M. daily June–Sept., 8 A.M.–7 P.M. daily Oct.–May), next to the Triple Bridge, not only offers maps and guidance, but is also the source for tours of the city. **Walking tours** (€7.50 per adult) depart twice daily (10 A.M. and 6 P.M.) between May and September, and on Friday, Saturday, and Sunday the rest of the year. You'll also find outposts of the tourist office at the bus and train stations (8 A.M.–10 P.M. daily June–Sept., 10 A.M.–7 P.M. Oct.–May) and the airport (11 A.M.–5:30 P.M. Mon.–Fri., 11 A.M.–4:30 P.M. Sat.). The tourist board also offers **bike tours** for groups of three or more from mid-April to the end of October. Tours should be booked ahead with the tourist office.

If your muscles have had more than enough, the tourist office has two more leisurely tours on the menu. **Boat rides** (€7.50 per adult) leave from Ribji trg pier near the Triple Bridge. For something even more panoramic, **hot air balloons** float across the surrounding countryside daily from March to September. Contact the Tourist Information Center for pricing and reservations.

Dial 981 for an **English-speaking operator** who should be able to help you with entertainment and events around Ljubljana.

BANKS AND CURRENCY EXCHANGE

Handling money in Ljubljana is easier than ever since Slovenia adopted the euro. If you need to change money, most any bank (Ljubljanska Banka is the major local bank) can swap your dollars for euros, probably at better rates than the hotels. ATMs all over town should work with your bank card.

INTERNET ACCESS AND COMMUNICATIONS

DrogArt Info Point (Kolodvorska 20, tel. 01/439-7270, www.drogart.org, 10 A.M.–6 P.M. Mon.–Fri., €3 for one hour) is conveniently located directly across from the train station. **Kiberpipa** (Kersnikova 4, www.kiberpipa.org, 10 A.M.–10 P.M. Mon.–Fri., free) has a few online computers and places to plug in a laptop. You can access the Internet 24 hours a day at the **City Hotel Turist** (Dalmatinova 15, tel. 01/234-9130, www.hotelturist.si). It's free, but there's only one station so it has a tendency to be in use. If you're really desperate, the two info points outside of the main **tourist office** on Prešerenov trg allow you to check email and send e-postcards free of charge.

LAUNDRY SERVICES

Chemo Express (Wolfova ulica 12, www.chemoexpress.com, tel. 01/251-4404, €10 for a load) can dry clean or wash your dirty clothes.

EMERGENCY SERVICES

The police can be reached by dialing 113; emergency info (ambulances and fire) is at 112. If your rental car is in distress, call 987 for roadside assistance. Minor medical emergencies

Ljubljana in winter

can be attended to at the Medical Center in Bohoričeva 4 (tel. 01/232-3060) or the Klinični center Ljubljana (Zaloška cesta 2, tel. 01/522-5050). The pharmacy Ljekarna Ljubljana (Prisojna ulica 7, tel. 01/230-6230) is open 24 hours a day, seven days a week.

Getting There and Around

GETTING THERE
Air

There are several carriers that fly into Ljubljana's Brnik airport (tel. 04/206-1981, www.lju-airport.si), 23 kilometers northwest of the center. Adria Airways (Gosposvetska 6, tel. 01/231-3312, www.adria.si) is Slovenia's national carrier, with flights to most major cities in Europe. Air France (www.airfrance.com) flies to Paris every day of the week, while EasyJet (www.easyjet.com) offers daily service to and from London.

From the airport, you can hop a city bus (departure at 10 past the hour Mon.–Fri., less frequent on weekends and holidays) or a taxi (stand in front of the terminal, tel. 04/206-1678, www.skokica.com, around €35 into town). There is also an airport shuttle, which costs around €10 and takes about 30 minutes into the city center. Call 040/887-766 for shuttle information.

Train

Railway travel isn't as glamorous as it once was, but traveling the tracks around Slovenia is reliable and relatively inexpensive. The station is conveniently located near the city center, a 10-to-15-minute trek to the main tourist sights. There are good international connections, and it's also a good way to see some other towns in Slovenia: Maribor (2.5 hours), Kamnik (1 hour), Postojna (1 hour), and Koper (2.5 hours) are all served by the train. Contact the railway station (Trg Osvobodilne fronte 6, tel.

Ljubljana's airport, 23 kilometers from the city center

01/291-3332, potnik.info@slo-zeleznice.si, www.slo-zeleznice.si) for timetables and more information.

Bus

The bus station (Trg Osvobodilne fronte 4, tel. 090-4230 or 01/234-4600, avtobusna.postaja@ap-ljubljana.si, www.ap-ljubljana.si) has both international and local connections and is a 10-to-15-minute walk to the city center. It is a safe and reliable means of getting around and connects to more locations than the train. You can connect to cities such as Škofja Loka (45 minutes), Lake Bohinj (2 hours), Kranjska Gora (2 hours), and Piran (2.75 hours).

Car

All highways in Slovenia (there are only one and a half anyway) lead to Ljubljana, so it's pretty much impossible to get lost if you're coming from another country. The highway to Zagreb (E70) takes you between the two capitals in about two hours depending on how fast you drive the 120-kilometer distance. Driving around Ljubljana is safe and, given that it's not too big, usually manageable for most every driver.

GETTING AROUND
Bus

City buses (Ljubljanski Potniški Promet, LPP, Trdinova 3 or Slovenska 55, tel. 01/434-3248, www.lpp.si) are a reliable means of getting around town if you're staying in the suburbs. Otherwise you won't really need them since Ljubljana's core is quite small and easily accessible on foot. The 22 bus lines run between 5 A.M. and 10:30 P.M., with a few operating until midnight and beyond. Tickets can be purchased onboard (€1) or from a newsstand or kiosk (look for signs advertising *žetoni,* or tokens, €0.70). A great deal for travelers in Ljubljana is the Ljubljana Card, offering free city transport, admission to museums and galleries, and savings at a number of restaurants, hotels, shops, and even taxi fares all over the city for 72 hours. The Ljubljana Card can be purchased online (www.visitljubljana.si) or from sales outlets around the city (such as the bus and train stations, tourist office, and many hotels) for €12.52.

Car

Major rental agencies such as Avis (www.avis-alpe.si) and Hertz (www.hertz.si) have outlets in Ljubljana. If you're driving around remember that blue zones allow parking for 30 minutes free of charge, while white zones allow you to park one hour with a parking ticket (€0.50, available at newsstands and kiosks).

Taxi

If you'd rather take a taxi, you'll find taxi stands outside the Best Western Slon Hotel, the railway station, close to Mestni trg, and on Prešernov trg (only at night). Each firm has different prices, though holders of the Ljubljana Card get a 20 percent discount from Rumeni Taxi (tel. 041/731-831).

Bicycle

Rent a bike in front of Café Maček (Krojaška 5, tel. 01/425-3791, €13 per day). The tourist office has also started a program to lend bikes from outlets all over the city (in front of the Slovenian Tourist Information Centee, Antiq Hotel, Ljubljana Railway Station, Ljubljana Resort, Grand Hotel Union Garni, Hostel Celica, Zlata ribica, M Hotel) from April through October (8 A.M.–7 P.M., 9 P.M. in July and Aug.) for only €1 (2 hours) or €5 (from two hours to one day). Ljubljana Card holders get four hours of free bicycle hire.

Around Ljubljana

IŠKI VINTGAR

Only 15 kilometers south from Ljubljana, a small rapid river forms a pretty spot for nature fans. A beautiful limestone gorge, filled with rapids and waterfalls and a ten-meter-high solitary rock formation dubbed the Rock Man, the Iški Vintgar gorge is a great place to go for hiking, with lots of trails, including the E6 European Foot Trail. Marked with white and blue signs, the trail will eventually link Italy, Austria, Slovenia, and Croatia.

The bus from Ljubljana takes between 30 minutes and one hour, depending on the number of stops.

RAKITNA

Thirty kilometers southwest from the capital, the small village of Rakitna has a nice Baroque church and the remains of a Roman defensive wall. The real draw here, though, is the sports on offer. In winter, the flat landscape makes for great cross-country skiing on the snowy karst plateau and ice skating on the lake, while in summer you can head there for a bit of swimming in the lake. The tourist association (Turistično društvo Rakitna, Rakitna Tourist Society, tel. 01/365-0082) can direct you to information regarding ski and skate rentals.

The bus from Ljubljana takes one hour.

ZBILJSKO JEZERO

Zbiljsko jezero, only 16 kilometers northwest of the capital, is the perfect day trip from Ljubljana. Here you can escape city hustle and bustle by renting a boat or carriage to tour around the peaceful lake, created in the 1950s. The lakeside village of Zbilje is much older, first mentioned in the 14th century. There's also a great hike following the 18th-century **Kalvarija** (Stations of the Cross), an uphill pilgrimage path dotted with over a dozen shrines.

The bus from Ljubljana takes 30 minutes.

STIČNA

Thirty-five kilometers southeast of Ljubljana, the **Stična Samostan** (Stična Monastery, Stična 17, tel. 01/787-7100, www.rkc.si/sticna, 8 A.M.–noon and 2–5 P.M. Tues.–Sat., 2–5 P.M. Sun., €4.50) only has a few full-time residents, but the cute Baroque church and the Slovenian Religious Museum (Slovenski Verski muzej) are nice for visiting if you have extra time. The Cistercian monastery is one of the oldest in Slovenia, dating from the 12th century, and resembles a castle more than a monastery due to fortifications to ward off the Turks in the 15th century. Especially of note here are the herbal teas, produced by the monks and nuns at the cloister, that claim to heal a variety of ailments. They make an interesting souvenir purchase.

The bus from Ljubljana takes one hour.

www.moon.com

DESTINATIONS | ACTIVITIES | BLOGS | MAPS | BOOKS

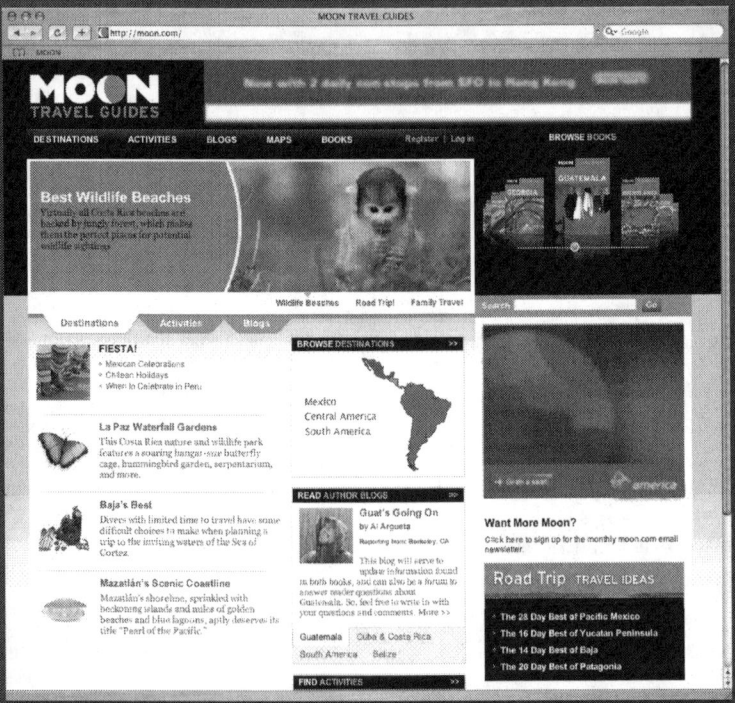

MOON.COM is all new, and ready to help plan your next trip! Filled with fresh trip ideas and strategies, author interviews, informative blogs, a detailed map library, and descriptions of all the Moon guidebooks, Moon.com is all you need to get out and explore the world—or even places in your own backyard. As always, when you travel with Moon, expect an experience that is uncommon and truly unique.

MAP SYMBOLS

▭▭▭ Expressway	◖ Highlight	✗ Airfield	⚐ Golf Course
▬▬▬ Primary Road	○ City/Town	✈ Airport	🅿 Parking Area
━━━ Secondary Road	◉ State Capital	▲ Mountain	▰ Archaeological Site
▫▫▫ Unpaved Road	✱ National Capital	✢ Unique Natural Feature	⛪ Church
----- Trail	★ Point of Interest		⛽ Gas Station
········· Ferry	• Accommodation	≋ Waterfall	◯ Glacier
⋈⋈⋈ Railroad	▼ Restaurant/Bar	♣ Park	Mangrove
▓▓▓ Pedestrian Walkway	■ Other Location	◉ Trailhead	Reef
⫼⫼⫼ Stairs	△ Campground	⛷ Skiing Area	Swamp

CONVERSION TABLES

°C = (°F - 32) / 1.8
°F = (°C x 1.8) + 32
1 inch = 2.54 centimeters (cm)
1 foot = 0.304 meters (m)
1 yard = 0.914 meters
1 mile = 1.6093 kilometers (km)
1 km = 0.6214 miles
1 fathom = 1.8288 m
1 chain = 20.1168 m
1 furlong = 201.168 m
1 acre = 0.4047 hectares
1 sq km = 100 hectares
1 sq mile = 2.59 square km
1 ounce = 28.35 grams
1 pound = 0.4536 kilograms
1 short ton = 0.90718 metric ton
1 short ton = 2,000 pounds
1 long ton = 1.016 metric tons
1 long ton = 2,240 pounds
1 metric ton = 1,000 kilograms
1 quart = 0.94635 liters
1 US gallon = 3.7854 liters
1 Imperial gallon = 4.5459 liters
1 nautical mile = 1.852 km

°FAHRENHEIT	°CELSIUS
230	110
220	100 WATER BOILS
210	
200	90
190	
180	80
170	
160	70
150	
140	60
130	
120	50
110	
100	40
90	
80	30
70	
60	20
50	
40	10
30	
20	0 WATER FREEZES
10	
0	-10
-10	
-20	-30
-30	
-40	-40

MOON ZAGREB & LJUBLJANA
Avalon Travel
a member of the Perseus Books Group
1700 Fourth Street
Berkeley, CA 94710, USA
www.moon.com

Editor and Series Manager: Kathryn Ettinger
Copy Editor: Amy Scott
Graphics Coordinator: Kathryn Osgood
Production Coordinator: Darren Alessi
Cover Designer: Kathryn Osgood
Map Editor: Brice Ticen
Cartographers: Kat Bennett, Chris Markiewicz
Proofreader: Julie Littman

ISBN-13: 978-1-59880-544-4

Text © 2009 by Shann Fountain Čulo.
Maps © 2009 by Avalon Travel.
All rights reserved.

Some photos and illustrations are used by permission and are the property of the original copyright owners.

Front cover photo: Ljubljana Dragon © dreamstime.com
titlepage photo: Ljubljana with bridge © Simon Krzic/dreamstime.com

Printed in the United States

Moon Spotlight and the Moon logo are the property of Avalon Travel. All other marks and logos depicted are the property of the original owners. All rights reserved. No part of this book may be translated or reproduced in any form, except brief extracts by a reviewer for the purpose of a review, without written permission of the copyright owner.

Although every effort was made to ensure that the information was correct at the time of going to press, the author and publisher do not assume and hereby disclaim any liability to any party for any loss or damage caused by errors, omissions, or any potential travel disruption due to labor or financial difficulty, whether such errors or omissions result from negligence, accident, or any other cause.

ABOUT THE AUTHOR

Shann Fountain Čulo

Born in South Carolina, Shann Fountain Čulo has been traveling all of her life. She studied abroad in both Spain and Germany and has visited 26 countries – many of them before age 21. She speaks Spanish, Croatian, and rapidly declining French.

After graduating from Sweet Briar College, Shann owned a multilingual staffing company, tried her hand at corporate gifts, and taught Spanish (with occasional travel sabbaticals in between) before becoming a writer. Now a full-time freelance writer, she is a frequent contributor to *Travel + Leisure* and *Condé Nast Traveler,* and her articles have also appeared in *Hemispheres, Four Seasons Hotels Magazine,* and several other publications.

Shann began visiting Eastern Europe in 1992, immediately falling in love with Croatia – and a tall Croatian as well. She made 16 Croatia trips in all, many of them for months at a time, until finally moving there in 2004. She lives in Zagreb, Croatia, with her husband (the tall Croatian) and their two young children. Writing this book, she fell in love with the region all over again, and became a wine connoisseur and an expert in traveling with kids. Shann spends her time writing, gardening, hiking, drinking coffee, and standing in line. That's Rule #4 of living in Croatia: Get used to bureaucracy.